Census

The Second
Seven Towers Anthology

A SEVEN TOWERS PUBLICATION

The Second Seven Towers Anthology
First published 2009
By
Seven Towers Agency, 4, St Mura's Terrace,
Strangford Road, East Wall, Dublin 3, Ireland.

www.seventowers.ie

ISBN Perfect Bound Edition 978-0-9562099-4-2

concept by Solid Design
www.soliddesign.ie
Cover, artwork, type and layout design and typesetting by
Seven Towers Agency
www.seventowers.ie

Printed by Genprint, Ireland.
Printed on 90gsm Muncken Bookwove White.

CONTENTS

Preface	5	Helen Dempsey	63
Introduction		POETRY	
Matthew Aquilone	9	Robert Donohue	67
POETRY		POETRY	
Liam Aungier	11	Susan Miller DuMars	69
POETRY		POETRY	
Joe Bacal	15	Sean Dunne	73
POETRY		POETRY	
Cleighton Blinn	19	Martin Egan	75
POETRY		POETRY	
Alma Brayden	21	Pauline Fayne	79
POETRY		POETRY	
Eileen Casey	25	Nicholas Friedman	81
STORY		POETRY	
Paul Casey	33	Ross Hattaway	83
POETRY		POETRY	
Seamus Cashman	39	Eoin Hegarty	85
POETRY		POETRY	
Patrick Chapman	41	Mike Igoe	87
POETRY		POETRY	
Grazyna Chludzinska	45	Andrej Kapor	91
POETRY		POETRY	
Steve Conway	51	Eileen Keane	95
STORY		STORY	
Anamaria Crowe Serrano	55	Neville Keery	101
POETRY		MEMOIR	
Catherine Ann Cullen	59	Noel King	105
POETRY		POETRY	

Lynne Knight POETRY	109	Maeve O'Sullivan Poetry	191
Quincy R Lehr POETRY	113	Karl Parkinson POETRY	195
Éamonn Lynskey POETRY	121	Emily Pepin POETRY	197
Hugh McFadden Poetry	129	Ray Pospisil POETRY	199
Orla Martin POETRY	135	Jane Robinson POETRY	203
Rachel Metcalfe POETRY	137	Jim Rooney POETRY	207
Donal Moloney STORY	139	Oran Ryan WORDS	209
Joe Moran PLAY	145	John W Sexton POETRY	215
Anne Morgan POETRY	155	Robert A Shakeshaft POETRY	219
Helena Mulkerns STORY	157	Barbara Smith POETRY	223
Rick Mullin POETRY	165	Oriane Stender STORY	227
Noel Ó Briain POETRY	169	Corey Switzer POETRY	231
Gréagóir Ó Dúill POETRY	173	Doog Wood POETRY	235
Fintan O'Higgins POETRY	177	Macdara Woods POETRY	237
Bernie O'Reilly POETRY	189		

Preface

All of the writers in this Anthology either read or had their work read at a Seven Towers reading event – Chapters and Verse Reading Series at Chapters Bookstore, Parnell St, Dublin 1, Ireland; Last Wednesday Series Reading and Open Mic at Cassidy's Bar, Westmoreland St, Dublin 2, Ireland; Last Wednesday Series Reading and Open Mic at Rocky Sullivan's. Red Hook, Brooklyn, New York.

This book is dedicated to the memory of Damian O'Brien who died tragically just before its publication. Damian helped bring about some of the events the works in this book are drawn from. We will always be grateful for and will always hold in fond memory his hard work and dedication as a professional and his warmth and enthusiasm as a person. Thank you Damian, and rest well.

Introduction

In a way, some of the readers of this book are unlucky.

I mean those of you who encounter for the first time the writers cushioned between the front and back flaps of the book you hold. Why? Because you don't know how they look; their hair, their eyes, the width and the length of them. You don't how they sound; their voice and accent, their confident
or shy intonation. All those human things that, combined with the quality of their art, made the performance by the writers of their work included here a thing to behold at Cassidy's of Westmoreland Street, on the last Wednesday of every month (bar one).

Of course, you didn't have to see the writers trade their wares in public to fully enjoy their craft as presented here. Each careful word or properly weighed paragraph is as open to enjoyment and understanding as any work published. Indeed, one could be tempted towards jealousy at the thought of the new experience of the first time reader. But to hear these words, to see the writers declaim them with measured tone or ironic detachment, where meaning can be conveyed by the writer's smile or the slow glide of a body across the stage — this is to know the writer, to know the writing in a very unique way.

This book is of course a record of things. Of these writer's thoughts and ideas, observations and insight? Certainly. A collection of the writings of those who have performed in front of a generous audience on the last Wednesday of the month? Definitely. A modest circumspection is probably the best approach to any claim to more. But what can be said, with absolute confidence, is that you hold in your hands a collection of fine writing, full of life, about living. For that, we are all very lucky.

Declan McLoughlin
December 2009

Matthew Aquilone

Matthew Aquilone is a poet and novelist from Brooklyn, New York. He is a Vassar University graduate in Art and a graduate of the NYU Masters Program in Creative Writing where he numbered Allen Ginsberg among his instructors. His work has been published in many journals including *Christopher St Magazine, RFD, Arkangel,* and *Otherrooms.com.* His play *Highest Perfect Wisdom* was performed in the Ensemble Theatre Octoberfest in 1996, and his short film *Easier Said than Done* was produced in 1998 under the auspices of Women make Moves/NYSCA. He has also won a number of awards, for his writing and his social work and is currently on the Board of Directors of the Housing Works Thrift Shop.

What kind of day is it?

What kind of day is it
Where there is only one poem
          At the end?

All day long
Bullshit. And you worry
Because who wants to lose a day?

At some point though you are resigned
And let yourself be taken by the world —
After all
It is the world which has granted you
The poem.

So you do her work, you
Sweep and pray and feed the animals
And when she's done with you
And you're cozy in bed
And you're thinking it wasn't such a bad day after all
And wouldn't be so bad were it this day everyday,

    If that's how things had to be,
    If there was no time or space or heart for poetry
    Despite how such a thought had frightened you before
    Despite what an empty, barren desert the prospect is
    Or how close it has taken you to doing yourself in —

Inspiration!
Like a drunken roommate
    Returns.

Liam Aungier

Liam is a poet from Co Kildare. He was twice runner up in the Patrick Kavanagh poetry competition. His debut collection *Apples in Winter* is published by Doghouse Books and he is currently qorking on his second collection.

Habitat

Where I first breathed life:
A long, low cottage with rafters
That groaned in the wind but never failed.
The threshold hollowed from use,
The windows modest and the mud-walls
Deep as the walls of any castle.
Rain and neglect have levelled it.
It is no-where.
It is everywhere I go.

****

Novelette

The Neva freezes over. Ice chimes
In Count Vorshinsky's glass. Under the stucco
Ceiling of his drawing room all Petersburg
Has gathered. Gossip bubbles like champagne. Cupids
Lounging in the plasterwork observe
Tatiana, who dances a gavotte with young Modest,
And notices Alexei notice her.
Snow decorates the city squares
Drifts and drifts across the endless steppe.

A footman yawns. A serpent clock strikes six.
The last guests depart. Tatiana offers
Her gloved hand to Alexei Kornakov,
Saying not adieu but au revoir.
Carriage wheels crush the glittering snow,
The solid river sparkles in the moonlight.
On the palace roof the snow begins to melt.

Tattoo

It's done so casually. He strolls into the shop
On some otherwise ordinary afternoon.
Words are spoken, an agreement made.

She suffers him to reveal the pale
Vellum of his shoulder. He sits for her
Inscrutable as a sphinx, and knows

Whatever she designs will be for keeps,
Each line, colour, letter or mistake
Is something he must carry all his days.

And yet he trusts her, doesn't even flinch
At the slight pain.
When she's finished he
Rolls down his sleeve, pays her and is gone,
From this day forth to live as her marked man.

Joe Bacal

Joe Bacal is a New York poet whose poems have appeared in several literary journals, including *Confrontation, Hanging Loose, Poetry New Zealand* and *Van Gogh's Ear.* He has lectured on creativity at the Parsons School of Design and is co-author of the satirical book, *How To Become A Legend In Your Own Lifetime—A New Concept in Self-Help.*

Canvas Dreams

Last year, after losing his job teaching art to four year olds,
Jake broke up with his sex and sushi girlfriend
and did something he had always wanted to do,
hole up in his skylighted fifth floor walkup,
painting ferociously, feverishly
splattering canvas after canvas,
his restless mind giving no quarter to time,
until, against his will,
he nodded off to REM sleep and dreamed
of Vermont and long lovely days painting
the swirling, changing colors and he dreamed
his landlord was banging on his door and dreamed
of the longing of lions and his landlord shouting,
"Don't pay the rent, I THROW YOU OUT!"
and he dreamed his sex and sushi girlfriend felt his forehead,
and it was hot,
and they knew it was more than sex and sushi,
and she got him his old job back,
and he showed the kids his paintings,
and they were silent,
and he cleared his throat and said, "Well?'
and Emily (his favorite) said, "Well what?
Who wouldn't like them?"
and Jake said, "Do you wish they were more realistic?"
and Emily said, "They're realistic to me. Just realistic
of a place I haven't seen yet,"
and Jake grinned so wide he thought his face would crack
and woke up to gray light and his landlord pounding
on his door with both fists and Jake turned over,
went back to sleep and dreamed his landlord
was dragging him out of his apartment.

Mom Could Talk to Anyone

She wanted to know why we were there.
She asked for water, Annie went to get it.
She said, *What is the point? Who I am
is no longer here.* She said, *Open
the window so I can jump out.* I started
for the window. She said, *Don't bother,
we're on the second floor. I'd probably
only hurt myself.*

When Annie came back, Mom changed
the subject, said there were three things
she wanted to do.
One. Go dancing.
Two. Eat spectacular food.
*Three. Meet someone wonderful
I've never met before.*

Well, who knows?
Maybe later. In heaven.
Lunching with God.
Gourmet Chinese food.
And late afternoon, a tea dance
with a small orchestra playing.
God would ask Mom to dance,
and as they waltzed around,
their feet off the ground,
she would say,
*You know, I've always liked that blue
you chose for the sky.*

Cleighton Blinn

Creighton Blinn is a New York based poet and reads at the Last Wednesday Series reading and Open mic in Red Hook in Brooklyn. His work has been published in *Down in the Dirt* (February 2009), *The Binnacle* and is forthcoming from Goldfish Press.

My Aunt Asleep

My Aunt is a rather proper woman:
Her hair always so neatly coiffed
That every strand stays in a prescribed place,
Matching the distinct modesty of her dress,
Plain garments of perhaps a generation ago,
Which declare her a lady
Uninterested in all that "nonsense."
This impression is reinforced by her chaste gestures,
And that voice of calm reason
With which she so typically speaks.

Yet if you observed her in her slumbers,
You might glimpse a hint of something else:
Visions haunting her senses,
Filling her mind with wild thoughts
Of caution tossed to the wind,
Revelling in the charm and humour of that old family friend,
Dear Mr. Reynolds,
Who no longer acts the pure gentleman,
My Aunt no longer holding her tongue,
Or acting in decorum,
Her body shifting restlessly in her sleep,
A smile spreading across her face,
Signs which will immediately vanish
Upon the light of dawn . . .

Alma Brayden

Alma Brayden is a well-known Dublin poet and artist. She is a member of Dalkey Writers' Workshop and has had poetry published in many anthologies and magazines. She has read her poetry on Abraxas Writers' CD and DVD, and broadcast on East Coast Radio and Lyric FM. Her first collection will be published by Seven Towers in 2009

Pythagoras in Love

How many ways
did he love her?
At a right angle
from his window
as she walked
through the square
of the hypotenuse
her proportions dazzled
his geometric eye
made up of numbers
his brain could purify.

Encompassed with fervour,
he composed love songs
full of mystical significance
on his seven string lyre,
wrote poetry, recited Homer,
went off regular solids,
became a vegetarian.
She was the centre
of his Cosmos,
the most beautiful
woman in Samos
his love was constant
as the morning
and evening star.

But she moved on
to the Semicircle,
blithely unaware
of his passion
leaving him lonely
in the sharp wind
blowing equally
from the squares
on the other two
sides of the town.

Killing the Light

Four fishermen lean
into the west wind
backs half-turned
from churn of sea,
boots pressed against
pool-wet sand,
big men, with broken
reflections of giants,
faces aged from salty gales,
sleeves rolled up their
oarsmens'arms,
weathered caps dipped
for a buffeting,
cable-stitched pullovers
faded to nothing.

At count of one
they grip their knotted nets
and pull in length on length
of silver salmon
in writhe and twist
of iridescence.
Green grasping waves
crash in to draw them back
in deadly tug-of-war

Their battle won,
the men stand back
wet-wounded, damp as fishes.
They smoke and count the catch
of flip and quiver-fin
whose waning scales display
ephemeral lights of all the oceans.

Eileen Casey

Eileen Casey is a winner of Maria Edgeworth, Cecil Day Lewis and Listowel Writers Week short story awards among others. She was also short listed for *Sunday Tribune* (first fiction) Hennessy Award, 2005. Her debut poetry collection *Drinking the Colour Blue* (New Island) was published in 2008. Eileen is a reader at the Chapters and Verse Lunchtime Readings.

Gull

'You should have seen it, out of her head she was.' Georgie is talking to Sara's left shoulder, the only part of her she can see in her mirror. If she tilts her head to one side she can see Sara's big round stomach, or if she leans closer into the glass she can see half of Sara's face. The left shoulder would do very nicely, she decides, then squeenches up her face as tight as she can to brush onto pale eyelashes her black mascara. Satisfied with the spiky effect, and in her own good time, she turns around to face Sara full on. 'You're really showing now, what does your Ma think?'

'Couldn't care less. Wants me out', Sara says, splaying out her hands, studying her chewed fingernails. ' Me and Davy will get a place off the social soon, and then I'll have lone parents to collect'. 'How can you be so sure,' Georgie asks.

'Course we'll get a place, Sandra and Jay got a flat the other day. We've got our names down ages.'
'If you can call three months ages,' Georgie says and laughs and then the laugh turns into a sharp cough.

Tell me again Georgie, think. Jesus, I can't believe that shite wouldn't melt in me mouth oul biddy said all that.

'She did, and more, only I can't remember every word'. It had happened so fast and Georgie's head was muzzy at the time from the cans. And all the cigarettes. 'About half ten it was. Me Ma and grand-da were in the kitchen'. Georgie begins circling her eyes with black kohl stick. All eyes and bleached hair, she is. It's the look she wants. Her mirror, surrounded by coloured bulbs, chisels into her skin a sickly yellow and orange tinge.

'You're just being a drama queen,' Sara says, in a needling tone. In her opinion Georgie has it made. Her mother fecked off and living with a fellah, not caring where Georgie goes. A Black man too no less, 'black as the ace of spades' her own ma who seen him with her own eyes describes him. Black men are very cool in Sara's opinion. 'No I'm not a fucking drama queen you fat fuck,' Georgie says with an edge in your voice. Sara squares back her shoulders and tosses back her ponytail.

'Where you off to today Georgie, into town again? Bet you're going off with Sam, or is it Mark?' She breaks into 'Georgie Georgie puddin' and pie, fucks the boys and makes them cry. Ah sure, you're the same as your oul one'.

Quick as lightning, Georgie launches herself off the chair onto Sara's swollen body. 'Shut up, shut,' she says. Before Sara can catch her breath she's pinned to the bed, her arms flailing, trying to pull

Georgie's hair as hard as she can. 'Fucking straw head, think you're great'. Sara's mouth curls in an ugly knot and a stream of curses snarl out as if they are breathing a life of their own.

'Slut, big fat fucking slut,' Georgie screams back at her. ' Bet that's not even Davy's'.

'Georgie, what's going on up there, come on now, quieten down'. Georgie's grand-da Noel stands at the bottom of the stairs, one hand holding the banister as if he needs it to stop him keeling over. Especially after the ructions of the night before. A neighbour knocking hell out of the front door wasn't the best way to end the day. Lucky for them the police weren't called. One minute Julie's telling him she's moving out for good and leaving Georgie, 'she'll be much better off here with you', and the next the front door is practically broken down with the pounding. Already there'd been a number of complaints from neighbours across the road. A house was robbed the week before, a car damaged. He never thought his neighbour would turn on him like that though. And like a crazy woman, furious with him and with Julie. 'The pair of you should be ashamed. Ruining that girl's chances . I should have have reported you to the social years ago,' she'd practically spit the words into Julie's face.

Upstairs, the racket from Georgie's bedroom grows louder. 'Georgie, Sara, give it over now. Jesus, have you no shame at all after last night? I don't want any more complaints.' He's hardly gotten any sleep, half-four and still looking at the clock. Then a fitful drifting in and out, and now he's exhausted and wants to lie down. He wishes Georgina was still alive. She'd know what to do. But his beloved Georgina is long dead. It seems like yesterday the doctor pulled him aside and gave it to him straight, 'I'm sorry, months at most'. Three months, that had been Georgina's allotted time. Three months and one week.

Overhead, the bedroom door opens and the two girls clump down the stairs, sullen-faced and tight lipped. Sara's hair is half in and half out of her ponytail, her face a livid red as if it has been slapped. Georgie, by contrast, seems paler than normal, the whiteness of her skin showing up the spots that have started to sprout. Malnourishment and smoking are beginning to leave their mark.

The thought makes his stomach churn. It's as if he is walking on eggshells all the time and can hardly recognise the quiet little girl Georgie had been. So long ago now, yet it's only been in the last eighteen months ago that the worm has turned. Dropping out of school after her junior cert, drinking, getting into trouble. And her lovely strawberry blonde hair, inherited from her grandmother, destroyed in one afternoon.

A bright child too, quick and smart. Always singing funny little rhymes. Especially when Julie was shouting the odds and doing her disappearing act. Pawning her daughter off with sweets and false promises.

'Sara's going home, she won't be stopping,' Georgie says through clenched teeth. Sara had gone over the line when she called Julie a good for nothing slapper. Nobody, but nobody will call her mother a slapper and get away with it.

Sara walks to the front gate and bangs it shut. She turns and gives the two finger salute to Georgie who, in turn, bangs the door as hard as can.

'You're well rid Georgie, she isn't a suitable companion, she's a bad sort,' Noel says. The tightness in his shoulders begins to unravel. Yet, deep down he knows there are other Sara's, the odds stacking up all the time. 'Grand-da, lend us twenty euros, I promised Lee-Anne I'd meet her in town'. Even though he's exhausted and would like nothing better than to lie down he says 'don't go out today Georgie, come on and I'll make you something to eat. There's sausages and some eggs.' The thought of the fry makes her stomach curdle. 'Nah, I'll get something in town, I fancy a burger'. She says 'buhgeh', losing the r's, her pronunciations getting lazier and lazier at each passing week. 'I'm sorry Georgie, I just haven't got that kind of money. I'm only getting a pension'.

'You don't want me to have any life, grand-da, give me the money, give me the money,' she repeats on a rising note. If she doesn't get out she'll faint and even though she feels rotten she wants a cigarette. Noel hates himself for doing it but he gives her ten. 'It's all I can spare and that's the last this week, now I mean it Georgie'. She grabs the money out of his hand and without a backward glance is out the door and heading towards the Luas. She takes out a cigarette from a battered package and clamps the slim white tube of tobacco between her lips. Her white fingers are already staining brown but she doesn't care.

Down the street she goes, the street she's grown up in, past the corner house with a crooked tree she swung around on a rope, up the hill towards the shopping centre, past the school she dropped out of. Overhead a gull chases a magpie and the two birds appear to be playing, dipping and diving through the air. She hears the quarrelling sounds and sees the bread in the magpie's mouth. The gull bumps the magpie's side like a joyrider on full throttle. The magpie doesn't put up much of a struggle and the bread falls down onto the grass. Swiftly, the gull swoops down and spears it. Soon, it is nothing more than a white speck as it goes further and further away. The school bell goes off as she passes and a knot forms in her belly. It's break time or a change in class. Her mouth tightens. Much better to be in town on the raz with Mark and Sam. She hasn't seen Lee-Anne in weeks. Reckons her ma is in hospital again. Or the oul fella in prison. She met Lee-Anne in Quirkey's slots around the same time as she met Mark and Sam. They were much more fun than stupid books and the stupid teachers. Sam and Mark were probably in Quirkey's by now, playing the slots, their eyes bright, their heads thrown back laughing. So far Georgie has resisted the small lump of white Mark keeps wrapped in foil. 'It's a fizz bomb' he says, 'go on, it's bleedin' great'. The first time he'd met her she'd been licking a lolly smothered in bitter sweet powder. She buys them with her smokes, loving the way the taste of the fizz explodes in her mouth. She says no to Mark's bomb, says she's happy with her cans and smokes.

The Luas snakes its way down past the canal towards Fatima and St. James' Hospital. Grandma Georgina died in there but from the Luas Georgie can't see that part of the hospital. She remembers the night it happened. How the neighbour next door took her in, gave her hot cocoa, put her to bed with a soft lamp left on. Then crying herself to sleep over grandma Georgina's death and wanting her own ma as well, wondering why she couldn't stay with her. Even though her ma was hardly ever around, Julie was still her princess and Georgie wanted her to be making the cocoa and turning down the bed and leaving the lamp on. But it hasn't been happening like that. As Georgie got older her mother seemed to grow more and more remote. Or had she always been like that? Going off on holidays without her, sending her postcards with a line or two on them which Georgie still keeps in her bedroom drawer. Places full of sunshine and palm trees. 'I could never take Georgie on holidays,' her ma'd say. 'She can't travel a mile without throwing up all over the place. It's best to leave her at home where I know she's safe'. Georgie doesn't remember being travel sick but she must have been or else her ma wouldn't have said so.

When the Luas stops at Heuston two druggies get on that she's seen around town a few times. They're well out of it. The woman of the pair sits across from Georgie while the man stays standing, holding onto the bar with one hand and a can in the other. There's two trailing wires coming out of his ears, the walkman tucked inside somewhere in his jacket. Over the bridge over the river Liffey the Luas goes, over a clump of gulls sitting on a lump of grey muck staring out into space. Not a care in the world only the next meal to worry about. The man's jerks as the Luas turns the corner, the metal snake bending into an accordion shape to accommodate the turn. Georgie looks at him from under her eyes. He is dressed respectably enough. A shock of red hair stands upright with gel or spit she can't tell which, his eyes are half closed, just a peep of blue because he is so out of it. Georgie wonders what he is listening to on his walkman or if it's turned on at all. At the next stop the door opens and he lurches forward. When it closes his yellow anorak gets caught. He retrieves it by jabbing at the door button, hit and missing it, and shouts out a 'fuck' loud enough for all to hear. The anorak is yellow and he is wearing brown trousers. Georgie stares down at his feet and sees that his runners have lights on the heels. They remind her of an airport runway. Grand-da Noel brought her out to the airport once to see Julie off on one of her holidays. Sometimes she'd go with a gang of mates, sometimes with a fella. It was night time and there was a strip of lights the whole way up the runway.

The man jerks forward again and drools a trail of vomit all over the Luas floor. It slides down under the seat near him, slip sliding along the floor. Georgie looks over at the woman who is chewing her nails. She notices that the woman's hands are caked with sores, especially the tips of her fingers. They are like the ones she sometimes gets around her own mouth. The skin on the woman's face is pock marked but her clothes are clean. The man leans over her and calls her babe. The woman calls him babe back but mutter under her breath 'fucking arsehole'. They lurch off the Luas at the next stop and when Georgie looks back at them she sees that the woman is leaning towards him and they kiss. The woman is kissing the mouth that has just spewed up vomit.

When Georgie gets off at Abbey Street and heads across to Dr Quirkey's Good Time Emporium she sees Mark on the slots inside the door. 'Hi, where's Sam' she greets him. 'He's still in bed, the lazy shite, me ma was about to throw water over him when I was leaving'. Georgie laughs. Things were looking up. She'd much rather have Mark on his own. Mark looks tired enough himself, very pale and there's dark rings circling his eyes. 'I'm a bit skint Georgie, let's go on the lift, we can flog the stuff down the flats'. 'Yeah, but let's get some cans first, I'm parched'. 'Yeah, okay, but you'll have to pay'.
Three cans later, Georgie and Mark are heading up an escalator in one of the department stores. Piped music floats over the store and Georgie feels warm and there's a buzz in her head. Mark's got the guts of €200   worth of jewellery in his pocket and she hasn't done so bad herself. A couple of good necklaces and earrings. They'll flog them in the flats and get at least a hundred for the lot. Plenty for a good night.

She feels dizzy too, remembering that she hasn't eaten yet. Still, the cider has gone straight to her head, exactly where she wants it to go. 'Mark, the minute we get rid of this, we'll have a blow out'. 'Fucking right,' he says back, 'just follow me, there's an exit by the jacks, just look cool'. Cool is Mark's middle name in Georgie's estimation. Mark walks ahead of her through the café area which leads to the exit. 'Come on, move a bit faster,' Mark says looking back over his shoulder. He just wants to get rid of the stuff in his pocket and get a hit off his contact in the flats. The place is busy but no-one seems to be minding them. They walk through a furniture section which is beside the café and as they do Georgie looks in the full length mirror on a wall in the middle of the floor. She sees her white face and her eyes red and rolling. She looks bombed alright and feels like laughing out loud. She can also see down to the middle of the shop where there's a couple sitting on a couch. Georgie can't be sure but she thinks she sees Julie and her fella bouncing on the leather, testing it for comfort. She leans into the mirror. Across the sea of couches and armchairs her mother looks up. Julie looks a bit startled at first as if caught in the headlights of a car but then she turns away and turns her back.

Her fella is leaning down to whisper something in her ear but Julie links his arm and pulls him away up the other side and they disappear. Georgie sees them leaving the space in the mirror, her mother like a big white gull, her white hair and her white coat beside her fella who is indeed black as the ace of spades, as Sara's mother has said. Georgie wonders if she has imagined them and thinks maybe she should chase back down the store and see if they're on the escalator. Her ma would like the jewellery. Georgie can see her being interested in them alright. Trying them on, preening. She'd take them from her, sure, but then what? What would happen then?

Georgie looks ahead to where Mark has reached the exit and is waiting for her. It looks to be all plain sailing now, they could be in the flats and have the stuff flogged in no time. Or, she could race after her ma, there was still time to catch her. But her stomach twists into a knot and there's a bitter sweet taste in her mouth. It's not the fizz bomb taste, but something else, something that threatens to lodge in her throat and choke her if she doesn't spit it out once and for all. She moves from the mirror and turns.

Paul Casey

Paul Casey was born in Cork, Ireland in 1968. He has lived in a number of countries in Europe and Africa working largely in film, multimedia and teaching. He began writing poetry in 1992 and has been reading and performing his work across Ireland and abroad since 2003. His poetry and reviews have been accepted for publication in a number of Irish journals including *The Shop, Revival, Cork Literary Review, Southword* and *Census*. A chapbook of his longer poems, 'It's not All Bad' was published by Heaventree Press in May 2009. He is the founder and organiser of the weekly Ó Bhéal poetry event in Cork, where he also gives poetry workshops, makes films and organises poetry events.

Painless

I'm at my new dentist with a loose crown
He holds up the X-Rayed future of my diet
an orthopantograph of secrets to chart
the teeth that shaped my every word

Upper right one bridge retained

Memory sinks into the trembling nuclei
of my own electricity, a shaman's drug
A ritual for visions and childhood seconds
Was ever pain the root of wisdom

Upper right two pontic of a bridge

He smiles Lipizzaner white
Well you've certainly been round the block
If only you knew Doc
what some horses have to go through
for extensive occlusal wear

Upper right three retainer of a bridge

At first appointments I open wide expecting shock
await for something like, *Jesus Christ Almighty!*
I muse on how they don't even blink
manage to avoid the right words

Upper right four M O D composite

His déjà-vu posture conjures
all of my very own dentists
flashing by now like needles
I can't remember exactly how many
yet only these strangers have ever seen
my thoughts this closely, could somehow
know me where most have not

Upper right five missing

I've been to so many dentists
that any nerves not removed
by pulpectomy have receded
up into the safety of my nostrils
perhaps even my eyes and brain

Upper right six crown

I remember beaming up at a dentist
in the Curragh when I was eight
thinking wow, women are dentists too
an upper brace for a crooked incisor, just great
no school though, here's to you

Upper right seven core and crown

The perfume of prosthetics, amalgam
of that pink moulding powder
and the faint but distinctive
superiority of dentist breath

Upper left one distal angle

Switch off my nose please
This time-chair reminds me
I've had so many root canals
that I don't need anaesthetic

Upper left two distal angle

I've always loved my teeth
though something in my sleep
would slowly grind the mind
with the adventures of sweets
How many nights dad would ease
a dollop of sacred whiskey
deep into an aching corner
to float me tearlessly away

Upper left three missing

I remember a Big City dentist
whose posture leant over me
at an angle slightly proportionate
to my health cover

Upper left four D O

Astutely aware of the minute hand movements
the variations in pressure
bracing for the jolt of steel
slamming into a nerve
Upper left five M O D and mobility

I exhume more buried treasure
A jackhammer vibrating brain cells
perhaps if I defeated pain then
I wouldn't have to feel it again

Lower left one to four present

Wishing for a masochism button, waiting
for that drill to burst right through my cheek
and beyond, when pain becomes a friend
something must be wrong

Lower left five M O D amalgam

There's good news though for one
who never used to speak much
as telepathic powers unfold
increase exponentially

Lower left six missing

For the frustration of not being free
to answer interesting conversation
unable to nod
primal sounds

Lower left seven M O

A country dentist who
for pocket change arranged
a root canal and abscess bonus
Rough dentists. Most were gentle enough
Lower right one to three present

A distracted dentist who while talking
of gold broke off the side of a wisdom
leaving me to swallow the blame
It was going anyway, never mind Doc
There's much more to worry about
out there

Lower right four missing

I've had the best
of entertainment from dentists
A tiny dentist lady who once
assumed an exotic yoga contortion
to extract a stubborn molar
knees and legs all over the place

Lower right five M O Mesial Buccal Composite

An up and close real live heroine
she was, piercing my fantasies
with the most clinical ice blue
a woman could ever offer
Now that's education

Lower right six missing

I would have made a great dentist
One thing I always found odd though
was the long drawn closeness of eyes
details only a lover should know

Lower right seven missing

They are all lost lovers, each an image
of fascination finely tattooed onto
a chronology of painless recollections
They're better than any psychologist
I've learned psychology from dentists

Lower right eight M O amalgam

As he finishes
I tip-tongue along
the peaks and crevices, valleys
of gum only Odysseus would dare

All these and more have witnessed
my sub molecular hero who celebrates
in slippery leaps from filling to crown
His triumphant emergence

His victorious trophy of mouthwash
They have traced my life as casually
as an old palm reader. I suddenly long
to thank each one with a bright embrace

Painless as an x-ray
I rise from the chair
gather all that care
inhale the light of day

Seamus Cashman

Seamus Cashman comes from Conna in County Cork. He founded Wolfhound Press, the leading Irish literary and cultural publishing house, in Dublin in 1974, and was publisher there until 2001. He had two well received poetry collections published, *Carnival* (Monarchline, 1988) and *Clowns & Acrobats* (Wolfhound Press, 2000) and his third collection, *That Morning will Come: New and Selected Poems* has just been published by Salmon.

The Wall

When you cross this pathway to enter
the woods, soft verge grass
imprints your passage;

concrete slabs that flank
your route, remain anonymous,
and you disappear.

There is hope
in teasing inner walls.
Impossibility

softens under a steady gaze.
So, scale with confidence that close
inevitable universe,

for in a moment's narrative
it parts. To claim the void,
emerge into its light.

****

Sometimes I am invisible

Sometimes I am invisible
to you. Then, only the elements
admit my presence.

Sometimes I am invisible
in the middle of a crowd
when I am shaping things,
and hearing the silent sounds
of nurture and seduction.
When words sit with me
and tell me who they are,
I hold them in my palms,
to absorb alternatives –
for doors might open
and turn my inside out.

Sometimes, hidden in the words of love
I am invisible to me
and wonder where I have gone.

Then my fear is that love will not await
the still moment between my heart beats
when I become visible again.

Patrick Chapman

Patrick Chapman was born in 1968. His poetry collections are *Jazztown* (Raven Arts, 1991), *The New Pornography* (Salmon, 1996), *Breaking Hearts and Traffic Lights* (Salmon, 2007), and *A Shopping Mall on Mars* (BlazeVOX, 2008). His fifth collection is due from Salmon in 2010. He has also written a book of short stories *The Wow Signal* (Bluechrome, 2007), an award-winning file *Burning the Bed* (2003), an audio play, *Doctor Who: Fear of the Daleks* (Big Finish, 2007), and episodes of the new children's TV show *Garth & Bey*. Patrick was the 2009 judge in the Over the Edge New Writer of the Year.

The Golden Age of Aviation

On his early transatlantic flights, he could smoke in the cabin
And drink as much as he liked and it was free although he wasn't even
In First. In those days, they didn't think about getting it in the alveoli
Because who knew then that cigarettes were evil; not to mention that
Everyone was in for it eventually, so why not enjoy the party?
It wasn't as though you could pop outside for a sneaky Camel Light.

Besides, there were other deadly activities that could be performed on
Aircraft, such as sex in the toilets; such as flying itself; such as hitting
A mountain or another plane. A UFO, should one pass by, was unlikely
To fry the controls with an electromagnetic pulse, but Armageddon
Might break out at any moment, because this was the nineteen-eighties
And there were oceans of oil on tap to fire up the engines of Pershings.

The cell-phone had not become popular yet and no one had digital devices
Which could interfere with the signals the nervous-system of the Boeing
Sent along itself to keep the great preposterous thing within its heavier-than-air
Suspension of disbelief – but there was always the chance that a Baader-
Meinhof splinter group might storm the cockpit and, with menaces,
Demand the pilot drop this bird in somewhere Communist and foreign.

The smoke from cigarettes of course detracted from the taste of airline food
Which, contrary to ill-informed opinion, was in fact delicious and quite good.

Athens Takedown

By a display of wooden penises,
Like acoustic vibrators,
In a flea market stall,
In the shadow of the Acropolis,
You compared one favourably with mine.
This did not hurt.

Not in this town,
Where riots set the streets ablaze;
Where Ancient Greece
Was shut because of strikes;
Where the police
Were shooting teenagers for practice.

Here, the windows of the Virgin
Blew cascades of album fragments.
The stone façades of banks
Burned black with cocktail evidence.
The headlines barely mentioned
That old Bettie Page was dead.

So when you gave me
Neil McCauley's speech from Heat,
I bought a wooden cock
And plastic worry beads for you,
Intuiting tthe uses you could put them to
Whenever you decidedit was time to walk away

Lux Aeterna

The light required to make a dawn
Is only the leavings of darkness
After it has had its way with us.

****

Manila Hemp

If I had been you –

I'd have checked the trapdoor and release
For proper operation. I'd have
Soaked and stretched the rope
To rule out spring or coiling. I'd have
Oiled the hangman's knot
For smoother sliding.

Tied around a grommet and a bracket,
The rope prepared to take the sudden
Weight and force of someone's fall;
Measurements, examinations, aiding
In avoiding strangulation or
Beheading –

That is how I would have done it.

But you were never me
And when you did it, you had no
Technique; you'd no finesse.

Your drop continued, feet-first, into
Other people's lives and through them,
Leaving exit wounds.

Grazyna Chludzinska

Grazyna Chludzinska is 29 years old and was born in Suwalki, Poland. She has been writing since 2004. She wrote a screenplay and directed it while volunteering in Finland. She has been working on *Thermos* a novel, written in Polish for the last few years.She has written a small number of short stories in English (*Cyclops' Sunglasses, One night in the Rio Scenarium* and *Short sleepless solitary*). She graduated the University of Economics in Poznan in 2004. She came to Dublin in December 2006 and works as a finance administrator. The following Story is by Grazyna,

The Cyclops' Sunglasses

The day that happened could not exist. It was a bomb in a catatonic shell. It happened for no reason. The day that Basil realized that the holes in his pockets are actually fortunate and sour milk in the fridge is tasty.

It began rather ordinarily...... Except for the strange smell of the cinnamon in the air. The cinnamon scent was somewhere between the duvet, then the cinnamon under the shower and finally it brought Basil's nose under the sofa and forced him to check all the pipes and air conditioning. He thought, 'Well, ok. No worries, I'll just explain it as a global warming effect; the heat creates weird creatures which carry stuff, in this case this bloody cinnamon, on their little hobbits legs. Don't panic. It's perfectly reasonable.'

He left the flat, started to walk and then it hit him. Not from the start though. There were no women on the streets...... He realized this when he passed the flower shop. There was no Deirdre there. Instead a young red haired man was cutting orchids. Later, on the way, he didn't see cute teenager offering free newspapers, whom he always teased, and there was no sign of Linda, the policewoman who used to walk the district every morning.

Basil thought that surely there must be some kind of a women's marathon in the city or a feminist's convention. Maybe all the girls, all the women are playing the new Wii Fit in their homes. Maybe they went abroad to look for unique organic cosmetics. Perhaps all ladies put on too much make up this morning which destroyed their look visibly, spent too much time in a solarium yesterday, dyed hair blue, green, gray (simultaneously)...

Honestly, he didn't care. It's not like he would miss them. At least for one day, he thought. Par example – his boss at the architecture office where he worked, was a Norwegian and was very demanding, she shouted, she bashed and swore like a scumbag. Basil's work mates think with one consent that she spent her childhood in strict Catholic school (strange for Protestant country), youth in a military collage and later worked at an oilrig somewhere at the Barents Sea. She was also 6'2" tall, had strong cheeks bones and short blond curls. Not to mention the evil, eagle eyed searching for an innocent victim's glance. Oh, yes she was exceptional; especially in the morning meetings she was possessed, throwing the pencils at subordinates and joking over and over about Luigi's tie. Basil hated those early tortures.

Anyway, today there's going to be none of that crap. It's going to be a piece of cake. Nice and easy.

Logan, his workmate, was talking about the Gaza conflict and Golden Globes at the same time. Then he switched to quitting smoking and taking anger management lessons (although he was very calm man). Basil was listening and was taking notes on the new project, which involved the construction of a new business plaza. He was preoccupied with the job, felt like porcupine in the desert. He considered himself as a rather satisfied person, but at work he just felt like he almost failed every time, and the more he worked the stronger the feeling was.

Huh, finally morning break. As there was no meeting earlier on, everybody took more than half an hour, some of the people went outside to cherish the fresh spring breeze. Basil and Logan stayed in the kitchen.

Basil was brewing fine grounded Arabica when he had a funny illusion. That is, he realized that next to them, stands Michael Jackson in person. He was wearing a surgeon's mask and was poorly trying to moon walk. He looked as if he was sliding on the green linoleum floor. Then he screamed something about Disneyland and disappeared. Basil sniffed his coffee and looked suspiciously at Logan. After all he might put something in his mug.

The windows in the office were half opened and you could hear birds' intense singing, the trees were vivid green and the sun was quite strong, fighting for space among cumulus clouds. Nobody seemed to be concerned by the fact that the women were missing. Nobody even spoke about them......

The day was going smoothly. Basil was drinking his coffee slowly, which was yummy and talked with Logan about his last trip to Chile, the subject that was never-ending. The other guys were making bets about Luigi's new car, which was Volvo S60; in how many years can it go without a breakdown.

Basil went to the loo. He was washing his hands when he heard following conversation.

"John, are you sure we're going to have a baby? I mean we are trying for six months now. Maybe it's the final time...... No, I bought the same test as usual. Hm? No, I checked in the calendar last time. It was two weeks ago... Ok, we'll go to the doc tomorrow. Don't get too excited John, we're still not one hundred percent sure. I'll talk to you later!"

Patrick came out of the toilet. He was quite thrilled. No, thought Basil, that can't be. Pat probably has a girlfriend, whom he calls John, that's some kind of freaky terminology. Nevertheless, he smelled that cinnamon again, which was a pleasant experience in a men's bathroom. This time he wasn't even bothered by it.

It was almost twelve and the architect nearly finished a big part of the project, and he was content, funny feeling, he thought, unusual but it felt right. Logan was mumbling something about flowers and gay relationship of his neighbors. Basil switched off as he wanted to end this before lunch. He was counting and making a prognosis. The rest can be done after the break.

Every day on their lunch break, Logan, Basil and two Chinese architects from the top floor were going to Java Café for salads, bagels or sandwiches; there was also fine selection of crêpes. Yin always ordered Cesar salad and mocha. His friend, Yao on the other hand, looked for the soup of the day, ham bagel and freshly squeezed orange juice. They were always talking in half English, exchanging the other half of sentences between each other in Chinese.

Anyhow, Basil looked at the big tv screen, the news was on. The news reader was talking about reducing global warming and the effect since The Revolution Day. Basil was curious about this weird revolt; he was surprised because he usually catches up with all the important news, he reads, he observes, he listens, he surfs but this one must have slipped away. He decided to investigate it at home.

After the lunch, Basil was even more into the work. However he was distracted once again when he noticed a crowd outside the window. Young men and teenagers were screaming something about release of a second genre and freedom of speech. They can't cut our throats, they chanted. The crowed moved on to next street and Basil returned to work. The hours flew by and he noticed that the cinnamon scent was replaced by the bergamot.

At last work was over and Logan first rushed to the exit, shouting to Basil something about a late beer tomorrow, playing darts and getting wasted. Oh, yeah, thought the architect, I almost forgot about that.......

The way home was bizarre, Basil was now more concerned with the missing good half of the nation. Nothing's changed since morning, and it should have.

He got back home. He began to feel dizzy, as if he had drunk five shots of vodka, which resembled him at Luigi's last wild birthday party when he tried to make out with striptease girl. He opened the window, and tried to take a few deep breaths. 'Easy man, easy, you're not going to throw up in the middle of the day, damn this low fat mayonnaise, I should have taken the salad without the dressing', he thought. Then he sniffed that bergamot aroma again and while he was looking out of the window, he saw a flying penguin that flew over the roofs and landed on the next building terrace and started to clean his feathers. 'Mutant' said Basil to himself and closed the window.

'I wish this day would come to an end. I wish all was like yesterday'. Then he remembered something about The Revolution Day. That must be the answer, he thought. The problem was that Basil was very tired, and still woozy, had no energy to search for any answer. He just felt like lying on the sofa and falling into deep, deep sleep.

He fell down on the couch, and closed his eyes immediately. Praying to wake up next day with the entire sweet feminine bunch beside him...

Steve Conway

Steve Conway is an Irish broadcaster and writer, formerly of the offshore pirate station Radio Caroline and most recently a presenter on the Dublin rock station Phantom 105.2. He started his radio career on a small London rock music pirate, South East Sound before moving to Radio Caroline in 1987, where he rose to the positions of Head of News and Programme Controller. In 1991 he was one of the final crew members rescued from the Caroline ship *Ross Revenge* when it ran aground on the Goodwin Sands. His memoir about his time on Radio Caroline, *Shiprocked, Life on the Waves with Radio Caroline* was published by Liberties Press in March 2009, to both popular and critical acclaim. He is currently working on his second book which combines a memoir from a different aspect of his life with an invitation for others to make their own memories.

Of Little Consequence

The saying that the flutter of a butterfly's wings can bring down an empire somewhere across the world implies that even the smallest of our actions can have untold consequence. But if this were true, then how could the revving of so many impatient engines be producing so little effect?

It was the summer of 1999, and the sun was baking down on the M25, making the hundreds of stationary cars seem to shimmer through a haze of petrol fumes. The motorway ahead of me could be seen falling and rising over the gently undulating Essex countryside for a mile distant, and there was not a movement anywhere. Or at least not in the anticlockwise direction – the cars on the other side were whizzing past speedily and smugly.

There were no roadworks ahead and, later, no sign of any accident or incident that could have caused the complete stoppage. The fact that the stoppage seemed so entirely without reason made it all the more frustrating.

I had been completely stationary for at least 10 minutes, and had long since switched off my engine, though many of the other drivers had yet to follow suit. The windows were down and my bare arm was trailing out and catching the August sunshine. It was impossible to relax though, as I had somewhere to be, a person to meet, something to be urgently collected and brought back to Southend, and I was already far too late. I would miss my looming deadline, the person would be gone, the consequences great from this inactivity.

After an indeterminate period, the glints of sunlight on cars far ahead in the distance began to move, slowly at first, and picking up pace, the wave of movement gradually coming back towards me over the mile of visible motorway. I started the engine in readiness, I would be moving in seconds.

And then I saw it.

A tiny movement out of the corner of my eye, a little green wriggling thing on the ashphalt ahead of me. I looked and saw it was a caterpillar, bound on a great journey from the grass of the central reservation across the traffic lanes and towards the verge and the lush green fields beyond. With everyone stopped, this little creature had managed to cross the outer lane of traffic, and had two more lanes and the hard shoulder to go. All around me cars were getting into gear, and the moving traffic zone was now only a hundred yards in front of me. Within seconds wheels would be rolling and the little green wriggling thing would never complete its journey.

I hesitated for half a second, and then, ignoring the startled looks and beeping horns of motorists around me, was out and onto the road, running between the other cars and vans to scoop up something that no one else could even see. The traffic was starting to move just 20 yards ahead as I dashed to the verge, gently lobbed the caterpillar as far into the hedgerow as I could, just making it back to the car as those around me started moving, but not before the driver behind had yelled something and waved his fist at me. And then I was driving, and within minutes the traffic on the M25 was back at full speed.

I can remember that I missed my important rendezvous, and that whatever it was that I was to collect and bring back to my shipmates at Southend went uncollected, but yet, the world kept on turning. Ten years later, I can't recall the exact nature of my mission, the identity of the person I was meeting, or the oh, so important item I had to collect. All that has gone, and the only thing that remains in memory now is the hot sun on the motorway, and little caterpillar that I helped on its journey.

I must have used a couple of gallons of petrol, and wasted several hours of my precious time on that eventually purposeless journey, yet I always remember it with a sense of achievement.

That little caterpillar was happy somewhere in a green field in Essex, never knowing of its brush with death, and who knows, perhaps there was a reason why the traffic had to be stopped, and I had to wait at that spot after all. Maybe this was the caterpillar that grew into a butterfly that one day flapped its wings and, in some far off land, brought down an empire.

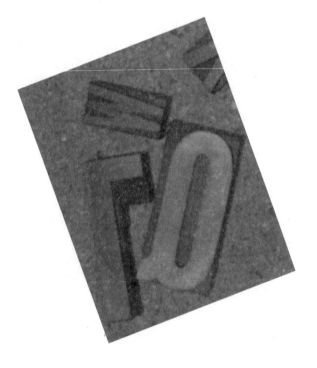

Anamaría Crowe Serrano

Anamaría Crowe Serrano is Irish and lives in Dublin with her family. She has worked at Dublin City University and Trinity College Dublin, and is currently a freelance translator and teacher of Spanish language. She has published several translations of poetry including Valerio Magrelli's *Instructions on How to Read a Newspaper* (Chelsea Editions, 2008). Other work includes a collection of short stories, *Dall'altra parte* (Leconte, Rome, 2003), a one-act play, *The Interpreter* (Delta3 Edizioni, 2003), and a collection of poems, *Paso Doble*, (Empiria, Rome, 2006) written as a poetic dialogue with the Italian poet Annamaria Ferramosca. Her first full length collection of poetry, *Femispheres*, was published by Shearsman, UK, in March 2008.

memory

for Sacha Abercorn and Kate Muldoon
on women's day 2009

deep within these stones
memory runs amuck
in its attempt to speak
                    and flow

its accent changes
with our comings and goings
ebbing through the earth
stumbling on the occasional lump
            in its throat
the odd scots or gaelic dyphthong
of a pebble colliding
with a blade of grass

we hear it gasp
and stutter in our sleep
though we cannot understand
                        a word
rooted as we are in the fixity
of things

the urge to be heard
sweeps the landscape softly
        like a flurry
                    lost
the moment it hits the ground

and this is all we have
by way of recollection
this air
        and space
lithographic wisdom now
no more than
whispers
through the waterlines

(first published in Osiris 68, *July 2009)*

open

the hills bow
ink blots
smudged against the sky
spelling understatement as they lumber
towards each other
to a point
defined by snow
as absence

what lies beneath –
broken land questioning its demarcation
is open
to interpretation

snow
punctuating silence
through the pass
intimating prose
ritual offering of the unspoken
to the shadows in the mind
that paint
a world rich in love and loss
where there is nothing at all

tulips

The tulips are splayed
letting go a posture that seemed
so pert
perfect
I would have said
some days ago.
They are stepping out of a pastel pose
a pink formality
that lent them classical airs
dinner party grace
and with age - just days -
burdened by beauty
they bow, relinquish
everything
to gravity
and sprawl through the startled
shadows in the hall
tango
from their tight-lipped centre
towards the wall
the stairs
the brush
of humans unaware
of the petalled voice
that only blooms
when broken

(from *Femispheres*)

Catherine Ann Cullen

Catherine Ann is a poet from Dublin. She is a regular contributor to RTE Radio 1's *Sunday Miscellany* and *A Living Word* as well as producing current affairs, arts and features. She lives with her partner Harry and daughter Stella in Kimmage, Dublin. Her first collection, *A Bone in My Throat*, is published by Doghouse Books in Kerry. Catherine Ann won the 2008 Francis Ledwidge Award.

Badger

I've never seen you alive:
You're from stories, riverbank tales
Of a gentleman in a dinner jacket,
The solid citizen who prevails.

A mystery like your name:
Are you badged head or corn-hoarder,
Or grey man, the Irish 'broc',
A fugitive living on the border?

Holing up in a dug-out,
Solitary or thick as thieves,
Covering miles in the night
To reach a safe house, eaves-
Dropping on your foes without a sound,
Giving no quarter when you clamp down.

Jazzy Surrey Sunday

It's Sunday and the Miles Davis Quintet
Is juggling The Surrey with the Fringe on Top
John Coltrane is flinging the notes into the air
When he takes us out in the surrey
When he takes us out in the sir-sir-sir
The surreal gig that takes to the sky
As though reindeer or unicorns
Were making us fly.

When he takes us out in
The saxophone with the fringe on top
The saxophone with the dinge on top
The lunatic fringe of the melody
Going on a binge of improv

Ain't no finer rig I'm a-thinkin',
It's a rickshaw, a jigsaw
Whose pieces float weightless in space,
Occasionally whirl near the original shape
Of the shiny little surrey,
Burst into smithereens.

When he takes us out in the surrey
The wheels are yellow
The feel is mellow
The dashboard's genuine hell for leather
We're riding in genuine heavenly weather
It's Oh what a beautiful morning
In the surrogate surrey with the fringe on the
top.

Helen Dempsey

Helen is from Rush in North County Dublin where she is a member
of a writers group. She has been writing for some time, and this is
her first publication.

Handwriters' Epitaph

In the tri-centenary of Joyce
queues will file past showcases
of long-hand manuscripts
wondering at a dead art

the rich and curious will pay
a scribe to execute
a hand-written note -
a peculiar, meaningless oddity -
like a hieroglyphic ornament

the flourishing language
of love will be lost in
abbreviations of a sim card

every child will learn to type
the universal encryption
globally accepted as the
currency of communication

the craft of calligraphy
will be bought on the
electronic market
endorsed by a personalised
holographic symbol

the envelope of surprises
filled with emotions
will be redundant
the font of sameness
extinguishing individuality

this is an epitaph for handwriters
the lost skill of materialising thought
shaped by culture and character
defining humanity replaced
by the word of an IT wizard
constricting our creativity

the oracles of antiquity
will be severed and silent
the writing on the wall
baffling the ignorant

MERRY - go - ROUND

RISE and SHOWER, DRESS for POWER

EAT a GRAIN-BAR in the CAR.

SQUEEZE into TRAFFIC-FLOW,

SCAN the PAPERS when it's SLOW.

Reach office
rev heart
phones demanding
markets start
paper piling
boss not smiling
clients complaining
heart straining
snacking
briefing
executive meeting
profits slowing
disapproval showing
submit plans for market growing
effectiveness waning
board disdaining
heart paining.

DRIP and BLEEP, REST and SLEEP

HEART DIED, END of RIDE.

Familiarity

we missed each other...
                    at the airport

you were looking for a red coat
                        I was in blue

there was a time when
you thought I stood
out from the crowd

we were younger then...
and love was fresh

now we have our
metallic award
for a generation together

like the papal blessing in the hall
you would notice
the rectangle of unfaded
wallpaper if removed

we are there for the long haul...
                    a familiar love

we laughed and hugged
when we found each other

Robert Donohue

Robert Donohue lives and works in Long Island, New York. His work has been previously published in *Measure, The Evansville Review* and *The Raintown Review.* He has also been nominated for a Pushcart Prize.

The Keats of Kentucky

Madison Cawein once compared
A New York skyscraper to a cataract.
He meant it as praise,
That a skyscraper was a fact of nature
And worthy of poetry.
The only reason he compared
It to a cataract
And not a rock
Or a squirrel's whiskers
Was that cataract
Rhymes with fact,
Which in the poetry business
Is now considered rhyme driven
And will not do.

But when the Twin Towers fell
They looked like they liquefied,
They looked like a cataract,
And an absurd story circulated
That a man surfed
All the way to safety
On a piece of debris.
So there you go.
Madison Cawein wrote this
About the Woolworth Building
In 1913
And at the time was considered to be
The Keats of Kentucky.

Susan Millar DuMars

Susan Millar DuMars is an American writer living in Galway. Her first poetry collection, *Big Pink Umbrella*, was published by Salmon in 2008. A follow-up, *Dreams for Breakfast*, will appear in 2010. Susan's poetry will also feature in a forthcoming Dedalus anthology of immigrant poetry written in Ireland; and in *The Best of Irish Poetry 2010*. She and her husband have organised the Over the Edge readings in Galway since 2003.

Winter, Eggs

In memory of Denice O'Neill, killed on Pan Am 103
over Lockerbie. She was twenty.

I thought of Denice
in the deli section of Atkin's Market
because she used to work there
(I saw her, for an instant,
under the fluorescence, in that stupid red
apron Mr. Atkins made her wear.)
And I thought, don't forget to call her,
and did I remember the eggs?

Walking uphill, into the wind,
hugging the groceries, scarred
and shrivelled apples from the orchard
underfoot. I'm trying to name the song
that was on the Muzak.
Thinking also of an omelette
and a strong cup of coffee.
A winter lunch.

Gretchen is waiting at the top of the driveway –
too pale, not waving, hugging her body,
where is her coat?
When I reach her, she tells me,
"Put down the groceries,"
so I balance them on the hood of a car.
"- something to tell you. Denice –"
Call her. Eggs. Got them.
" – was on that plane. That we saw
on the news."

Grass on fire.
Seatbelts hanging from trees.
The groceries start to slide.
Gretchen steadies them.
My voice is like ice creaking
and shattering under our feet.

I remember.
The song on the Muzak was "Fire and Rain",
and I saw her, for an instant,
her brown arms on the counter,
giggling with me about Hank Armstrong.
Asking if I wanted to go swimming
at the reservoir, when she got off work.
But that was summer.
We are deep in winter now.
The reservoir is silent, choked with ice.
I remembered the eggs, and I came home
and next I would have called her.

We head inside. Gretchen carries
the groceries.
Later, she puts them away.
Snowy white eggs, whole and perfect.
Safely away in the refrigerator.

****

Poets Are Just Like Everyone Else

Today over breakfast
Husband and I discussed
the rhyme scheme of Petrarchan
sonnets –
its merits, relative to
the Shakespearean style.

I sipped my cappuccino
thoughtfully.
Husband stroked
our cat.
It was an edifying
conversation.

After which, Husband and I
scaled the drapes
and batted at invisible
birds.

Our cat sighed,
tidied his whiskers and
kept reading the Guardian.

****

To Sylvia Plath

I mistook your
open graves
for cathedrals.

Paid my pennies
and lit candles inside.
I thought you were
very brave.

At twenty-nine I tried to die.
Shredded by my need
for work that mattered, clothes that fit,
a face glad to see me.

This need had no dignity –
lay naked,
legs spread,
howled and stank.

Maybe I did die,
to be wombed in the cabin of a jet,
its landing screech and jolt
my birth cry.

Learning to walk the second time
is harder.
I can't forget how it hurts
to fall.

I've come back to myself,
someone else.
I think I am
very brave.

Sean Dunne

Sean Dunne was a poet from Waterford City. He was born in 1956 and died in 1995. He attended Mount Sion primary and secondary schools in Waterford City where he began his career writing for the school magazine. After graduating from UCC he settled in Cork where he worked in the city library and became a columnist in the Cork Examiner daily newspaper. He published three collections of poetry, *Against the Storm, The Sheltered Nest* and *Time and the Island,* as well as editing a number of anthologies.

The poem that follows was given as a gift by Sean Dunne to Lucy Glendinning. The poem was read for the first time at the Sean Dunne Festival in 2009, and had not been heard by his family or published before.

****

Lucy Glendinning

Lucy Glendinning was born in Cork and educated in Scoil Mhuire, Cork City and subsequently in Mount St Michael's Convent of Mercy in Rosscarbery. Her maths teacher, Des Gloster, was a close friend of Sean Dunne's and introduced her to Sean who gave her the poem 'Wood Quay, Reversed' during one of many social occasions out with the sixth year students. Lucy kept and cherished the poem and was delighted to bring its existence to the attention of the organisers of the festival in Waterford that celebrated Sean Dunne's life and work. She now lives in Kilkenny with her husband and three children.

Wood Quay, Reversed

Sic Sitric Dixit:
Their faces were never rugged and raw
As a seaboard winter, and their hands
Had hacked no rock or stone but knew
Only softer things - a glove's comfort,
Annual reports, alderman's robes.

What flowers they knew were casual
And nameless, occasional as the sky
On kitchen calendars. For them the sea
Never swelled with Gods of gale and calm
But lapped in August on brochure beaches.

And their songs, their books, were momentary
Wonders, untouched by poet's or singer's tongue
In the old celebration of earth and stars.
Their world in tins, their readymade lives
Were instant as death, and as predictable.

So let us preserve this patch of their world
And measure our lives against its ruins.
And when with your children you walk
Walk carefully, for you walk on bones of the dead,

You walk on tins.

Martin Egan

Martin Egan is a writer, poet, playwright, painter, performer and musician. He has just made *The Tune,* an Unreleased Album covering the years 1992-1997, recorded with Donal Lunny, Don Baker, Davy Byrne, Keith Donald and the late Jimmy Faulkner (available for Download at www.martinaegan.com). He will be releasing the Album also in a Limited Edition C.D. Format on March 5th 2010. A brand new Martin A. Egan Album will follow in late 2010 on his own Label. Martin has been performing professionally since 1970 and has performed at the early Glastonbury Festivals and shared stages with The 101er's, who became The Clash, with Steve Winwood, Here and Now, Steve Hillage, Hawkwind, Gong, Kilburn and the High Roads (Ian Dury) and numerous other U.K. and Irish Acts. Among his many songwriting credits are "Bishop Casey" one of the tracks on Christy Moore's biggest selling album *Live from the Point,* which spent 16 weeks at Number 1 in 1996. Achieving Multi-Platinum Status in Ireland and Mainland Europe twice with Christy Moore in 1996 and 2006 he was nominated for the German Music Award in 1997 with Mary O'Regan of Draíocht for her solo album on which he wrote the title track "Every Punch Needs a Kiss", as well as three other tracks. Since returning to live performance, Martin has become well known on the Dublin reading and open mic scene as well as returning to Live Music Performance.

Muse crawls about the floor
Of a North Beach skid row bar
Full of known criminals, drunks,
Punks and junkies who are
Dumping drinks down slowly
Knowingly lengthily ending
The lives of their muses, boozers
Slaves to miserly misery, slit eyed,
Nursing the last shot, watching
The door each one of them uses
It leads to dirty toilets full of spoons,
Black-backed, discarded lighters
Dirty needles, rusting on the floor
Muse rubs her face in spit and gum
Eats sawdust and in an alcoholic fit
Begins to howl like a million babies
Swaddled in discarded condoms
Passes out in the vomit and come
And nobody particularly
Gives a fuck
No-one even looks up
The silence is only
Ever broken by the sound
Of a million dreams washing
Down the flush
A guy farts and leaves
Stepping over Muse
As she sleeps
Her dreamless sleep.

This poem is the wrong shape
To be cool, to fit the page
To engage the spirit of
The eternal watery flow
Known as muse, its
A muscle-less muse
Muse-like came of music
Music came of muse
Amusement stepped sideways
From her and fell over laughing
In a troubadours jingling hat

****

The older I get the more my limitations
Step on my fingers and hold me freezing
The room of my mind fills up with ice
Moving in and up and sideways too
All over its walls the floors the ceiling
Misty faced bodies suspended receding
Effulging yet remaining, frozen, distant
How like my Father I'm becoming
I am too far from him to walk in
On him talking about things and people
No one in my entire family knows
Places and things they have never seen
Are familiar to me as my Mothers picture
Sitting on my rented mantel smiling
I wonder how she looks in his frozen brain
In what decade are he and she dancing,
 Early forties, Late forties, early fifties,
Jitterbug, Bunny Hug or strict time ceili
No one smiles the truth into a camera lens
They're always on their guard or else
Hamming it up with the best of them
Or with an eye to the future viewer
My Mother was always like that, severe
Strongly formal, a stiff and sober tyro
Or the drunken life and soul of parties
They were made for each other
My Father and Mother,
In each others memories

Edna St. Vincent Millay is sitting side by side
With Freya Lawrence and Georgia O'Keefe
With my middling mother's ghost muddling
Mad as a Marching Season in their midst
The hands that wrote the music, fingers
Broken
The tongue that tore the skin of others,
Cold
The voice that sang the melodies, no longer choking
Out a sentence " Let me alone I am old, "
The words that broke the bones with cruel vowels
Foulness and imprecation, desperations spoken
Tone
Yoko Ono silent, in her dark Dakota tower,
Breathing endless loss over fragile glassy flowers
Emmie Pankhurst crying softly weeping, "Freedom"
Her bleeding head and hands lace up corsets
Unyoking,
My Mother drunk and sitting at the feet of Helen Keller,
Tapping rhythm on a table with Cinderella's stolen slipper,
Silenced into photographs, relicts of museums, all are now
Reposit'ries of thought and loss, of dying colours

Pauline Fayne

Pauline Fayne was born in 1954 and lives in Tallaght, Co. Dublin. Her first collection *Journey* was published in 1979 by Sheveck Press. Her second collection *Killer of Fishes* was published by Stonebridge Publications in 2001. A third collection *I'm Fine, Really* was published by Stonebridge Publications in October 2005. Her fourth collection *Mowing in the Dark* will be published by Stonebridge in 2010. Pauline's work has been included in several anthologies, including: *The White Page* (edited by Joan Mc Breen and published by Salmon Press); *Four Urban Voices* (edited by Dermot Bolger and published by Raven Arts Press); *Rainbows and Stone* (edited by Michael Bouchier and published by Real Ireland). Her work has also been broadcast on RTE Radio 1 and BBC Radio 4.

Copy Cat

She mimes each motherly move
learns the wordless tunes
the occasional
impatient
toss of the head

flings her baby doll high
until its voice box growls
with plastic laughter

and at bedtime
carefully lathers shampoo
into its stiff eyelashes

soon she will be old enough
to hold the iron.

Nicholas Friedman

Nicholas Friedman is a native and current resident of Syracuse, NY.
He works as assistant editor of The Barefoot Muse, an online journal
of formal and metrical verse. His poetry has appeared or is forthcoming
in journals such as *Measure, LIGHT Quarterly, The Annals of Internal
Medicine, The Raintown Review*, and *Blue Unicorn*.

Scenes from the Psychic Fair

Whirling from their seven chakra faults,
Etheric double-men parade unseen
In subtle shades of indigo and green
And drift into a spiritual waltz.

From each refulgent aura's layered screen
Spring astral orbs like budding cosmic pimples,
Defying any being's being simple.
Sans prods and nodes, a Kirlian machine

Unleashes its electrographic wimple
Through my pristine skin. Now, still alive,
(And having paid a modest twenty-five),
I'm handed back a photo: red cheeks crimpled

By a leery smile hep to cosmic jive,
And eyes cast sidelong toward some hidden judge
Who coyly waits to give the wink and nudge—
It's bunk! Your money's better spent in dives!

But in the picture looms a blackened smudge
That bodes of karmic debts as yet outstanding.
The judge is no apostate! He's remanding
Skeptic souls until they've made the budge

Toward revelation. Notwithstanding
These initial barriers to faith,
My Manipura urges me to bathe
In deva's healing streams. With senses banding,

I'll fix myself a lodge inside the Eighth
House walls, then tame unruly Muladhara
With this newly revamped Sahasrara,
And dance a fox-trot with my glowing wraith.

Ross Hattaway

Ross Hattaway was born in New Zealand and has lived in Ireland since 1990. He has published poetry in periodicals and collections, including *Writings* (Wellington), *Life Beyond the Louvres* (Northern Territory Anthology), *Poetry Australia* and *The Raintown Review'*. His readings include the *Poetry Ireland* Introduction Series, Anna Livia FM, Between the Lines (Belfast), Chapter and Verse, the Last Wednesday Series, Ó Bhéal and The White House Poets. His first collection of poetry, *The Gentle Art of Rotting,* was published by Seven Towers in 2006 and he is currently working on his second collection. In 2008 Ross was a guest at the Poetry Spring Festival in Lithuania, becoming the first Irish poet to guest at that festival. Part of The Gentle Art of Rotting was translated into Lithuanian and published as part of the festival celebration. Also in 2008, Ross was a guest of the Live Poet's Society in Sydney. In 2009 Ross was a guest reader at the Saturn Sessions in New York.

Black and Tanka

Demonise. Sometimes
all we see are demon eyes
when the mirror should
show us the one thing, ourselves,
and we really don't get it.

Counter Tanka

Every sound counts,
as sweet as. Tap a line like
tapping kegs, put that
tap hand up and give me five
seven five seven seven.

Feast of the Assumptions

You say
the land is water
but we walk
and we walk.
That the land is butter
but it is not
fairly spread.
That it is mother and source
but we cut it and burn it.
We seed it.
Bottomless
but still we dig
for foundation, for purchase.

I come from sky and water
and light holding down the water,
horizons holding down
the sea.
Fishing can be my digging.
Here is my line.
I'll eat with it.

Eoin Hegarty

Eoin Hegarty is a teacher, based in Fairview in Dublin. He has been writing poetry for some time and is a regular reader at the Last Wednesday Series.

Autumn Prayers

Leaf rubbings
in thick childish crayon
Or angled pencil -
a frantic conjuring
at the image

and the constant appearing –

chestnut veins
lines of sycamore
maple leaves and the edges
of the small rowen

in real delineation

A prayer in heated
weavings
And all round imagining
transplanted colours
or lines of grey

and the slow emerging
Water forward now
Through the white paper

spiritus
pressed to a leaf print

like something of itself
called and held
 in the simple act of naming.

Mike Igoe

Mike Igoe is a performance poet, well known on the Dublin reading, performance and open mic scene. He has run a number of events around Dublin and currently runs the Naked Lunch event in Féile on every other Wednesday.

Concrete Donkey

I'm tired of the head shops, body shops and office blocks,
Knocking shops of the emotionally null and void,
Inscrutable paranoids stabbing pens at flat screen monitors and
Pulling monkey faces at Monday morning perculators,
Fuck me it was bad this morning,
I keep dreaming I'm going back to the kill floor,
Staggering under the lasers, meaning something to somebody,
Dust onto dust. When there's enough vodka flowing,
We start dancing; slowly at first, self-consciously,
Nobody looking at anybody directly,
All trying to appear happy,
But the drink flows and we start to kinda feel happy,
Despite ourselves, despite the dirt of it,
Laughing in the empty face of it,
Tearing through each others scarves and jackets,
Sweat drenching our skins, our whole bodies
Tingling with the grime of some strange and brutal joy,
Grimacing and touching, throats fucked, sweet nothings,
Black out to orgasm...

(Nun scheint in vollem Glanze der Himmel)

In the sensory jungle of the floor an angel is propagating thought
stems of *Howl* and *Psycle Sluts*
To the *illiterati* on either side, who shriek and shit themselves, he just
hugs them,
He looks strung out; Loose fitting T-Shirt, lynxed and smiling,
Sweat dripping from his fringe and on his forehead,
Red-raw incandescense of body heat and white light
He rode right into the parted flood of the floor
On a whip-sore blood-matted saintly ass,
A poutin' proud and sturdy ass;

SLAP

He remakes the world for me; the tapestry in the Central Bank
Is rent in twain, a formless black hex thing blots the skyline
Over Sandyford Industrial Estate; Trams arrive six hours late,
Concrete Donkey descends, hurtling out of the God void

With rectal fanfare and malignant pornographic grimace;
Terrible billion tonne retributional albatross,
Bone crunching terror-thing of critical mass,
Ate is riding him side-saddle, crack addled, bearing
The scales of justice, a crosier, and a suggestive riding crop;
Screaming in Enoch, *'I'll rapture the lot a yeh! Avert yeer fuckin'*
eyes!'
Children with no politics try to rise for the national anthem
But are restrained by spectral man corsets
Already a thousand years old and tired of dialogue
Unilateral trumpets recite John Philip Sousa's *Liberty Bell*
There's a smell of shite and burnt hair searing what dignity
remains
From the spent and speechless millions, brains finally fried,
Masturbating half-hearted, watching television,
Cum-faced in oblivion.

(Vollendet ist das große Werk)

Lyric of What We Might Do Tonight

Let us drink up the nectar of a thousand honeysuckle vendors,
Let us sup the pure animal fervour of the hemlock maiden's jugs
And fall on the floor and make love to the furniture.

Let us bicker unto an endless point in the beer gardens of Dublin,
With our eyes cocked in every direction at the men and women who pass
All our dreams of bodily juices infinitely possible in our heads.

Let us wish we were dead on the floors of bedrooms with rotten threads of
Soiled tissues and coffee cups with a layer of scum,
From Ballybrack to kingdom come
Let us climb back out of our graves and thumb lifts to unknown quantities,
And, surpassing the uncertainties of city midnight,
Take taxi rides to pointless suburbs on the laps of much older men
Let us bring them to ecstasy in the moaning heart beat of the morning
And leave them breathless setting out for the first dart to Tara Street
Back to the flat for more weed and drink and philosophy
And hideous sodomy beneath the stairs.

Let us lie on our backs to eyeball the stars
Lullabies in our hearts for our drowsy lovers
Stretched out in gutters, crowned with constellations,
Let us rend the gloom shrouds of perception
With our sensitive meat and chemical box cutters
And slit the necks of whatever wizards wait beyond.

Andrej Kapor

Andrej Kapor is a poet originally from Croatia and now based in Dublin. He is very well known on the Dublin performance and reading scene and has performed at many major events, including the Electric Picnic.

Where the Willow Grows Aslant

Sound of kisses
Dropping
In the stillness of the bay
Where drowning victims washed ashore

In my dreams you never talk about existence
Or the boys with whom you used to dance;
In my dreams you never talk
Anymore.

Have you seen the moon, my dear?
Tonight, it smiled at me;
Thought I'd grace it with some lunatic verse.

I played with paupers in the gutters.
They laughed at my lost years.
I ran home
I locked the door
And I strung out my holy curse.

When the Witnesses are Gone

I have built you out of longing
And I wrapped you in the cold
And I raised you on a pedestal of pain.

But you were screaming like an angel in the place of no surrender
I carved a future on your back
And took what was not mine to take

Now the seasons slow my heartbeat
And my mouth is running dry
But you know me;

Endlessly curious, yet never quite so brave
To tell you just how beautifully you ache.

****

Lautari

Listen to silence
A heavy tread upon your soul,
It breaks you where you stand.
Black-clad angels dance the tango
Until they've all gone mad.

Their laughter, and the rusty strings of violins;
You are slipping through their music.

Candles are melting.
Walls are made of yellow paper.
It is dirt that they are sweating.
The air is getting heavy.

Let the angels bathe.

Eileen Keane

Eileen Keane's first short story won the Cecil Day Lewis fiction prize in 2004 and in 2007 her short story *Tryst* was one of 14 chosen through a competition on Seoige and O'Shea on RTE or an anthology called *Do the Write Thing* (Poolbeg Press). In 2008 she won first prize in the humorous essay competition at Listowel. In 2008, her story *The Cave* was published *in Census, the First Seven Towers Anthology*. She is a visual artist, a member of K.A. (Kildare Artists), Clane Writer's Group and a founder member of the Leinster Printmaking Studio at Clane, Co. Kildare and has just completed her first novel.

Woman Walking on Nassau Street

That woman on Nassau street. Her image on the screen of my mind like some subliminal messaging system. I saw her yesterday, not long after I arrived here in the city. I keep coming back to it, why she stood out from all the others, the incongruity of her clothes and makeup.

I've been wandering the city, looking at buildings, people, that river. I'm trying to make sense of it, why I left home, what I'm here for.

I could make a list, I suppose, of things that might have had a say in it all. Fliers in the door about night courses, headlines about banks failing, talk of recession, a streak of blue dye from Dan's shirt on the front of a blouse I loved. Or the trees everywhere dying off, flinging their ragged leaves down around the gardens; the empty houses in the estate stolidly waiting for the slump to be over so that they can breathe again; the small town feeling of nothing new, like being in an eternal conversation where you know the ending but have to go through the steps to arrive there, over and over again.

If I told it a different way you might think that it all hinged on the portrait of my aunt. Because it was that that finally made me walk out the door. It wasn't a rational decision. I stuck the picture in my handbag, picked up my coat, and left. I have the picture in my bag still. I look at it from time to time. It's not that I expect answers exactly, it's more like a point of departure for the thoughts that spread outwards from there like a complicated mind map with spaghetti strands criss-crossing and tangling from one thing to another.

What is striking first is the perfect stillness, not the momentary inactivity of maintaining a pose, but rather an air of stillness that pervades the whole thing like in the portrait of the Mona Lisa or Lady Lavery, or some society lady. Her beauty, maybe that's what gives it that air, of the perfect thing, the finished product. There's something universal about it. It's a black and white photograph; her hair is wavy and worn short, swept away from her face to expose a high forehead. She's wearing a dress with a v-neck and a collar with a ruffled edge. Her complexion is smooth, with high cheekbones. I imagine the creaminess of her skin, the roseblush cheeks, a slash of red lipstick the only makeup she'd have worn. And that's the image I want to keep, her face half turned to the camera, her folded hands, her confident gaze.

I imagine her in her best dress, her hair carefully curled and set and loosely protected by a patterned headscarf, giggling with my mother as they cycle to town. A special trip to get the picture taken. She's 19, my mother 23. And then my mother helping her, fixing her collar, her hair. That calmness, that gravity, that certainty of all that is due to her.

My mind flicks over to the other woman, the one I saw on Nassau Street. I couldn't take my eyes off her either. But it wasn't her face that brought her to my attention at first. She was ahead of me on the street, striding purposefully along. She stood out from among the others, hundreds of them it seemed to me, jostling each other in their hurry. What was striking about her was that her body didn't fit into the picture that she had created of herself, or at least not conventionally so. Beautiful straight long black hair, trendy clothes, but all wrong for her, too many bulges, too much flesh distorting the shape of them. Pretty skimpy wisps of fabric made for lithe bodies, pretty young girls. She screamed inappropriateness. I should have left it at that but some perverse curiosity prompted me to pass her, to look back. To see if the picture she had created on the other side fitted better into the mould. And when I saw her I was really shocked at first, and ashamed of having followed my voyeuristic whim, but yet drawn to look again as if to confirm her ugliness, which was startling. And her face keeps coming back to me, like a sore on my arm or leg that I can't stop myself from worrying.

Perhaps it was because the story of my aunt was playing on my mind, the contrast.

When I knew her, her beauty had faded, hidden behind worry lines and cheap clothes and a husband who saw only his own reflection in the mirror the world held out to him. A life spent caring for others. As if she had settled for second best, for a life of compromise, though her portrait showed her hopes and dreams. Maybe things would have turned out differently if she had had children of her own.

When I cleared out her house everything went into the skip. She had acquired nothing of value in the end. Just one small box of things to keep. And when I spread them out on the table in my kitchen on Tuesday and found the portrait in an old letter from my mother, I didn't expect that it would lead to this. They're probably still there, the other things, still innocently cluttering my table. The kitchen is a foreign country to Dan, after all.

That picture. I want it to release me from the other images, the last ones, the final one that won't let go: her withered skin like parchment against the stark white pillow, the hollows in her cheeks, the vacant eyes. If I had a series of pictures from her life, you could observe it, the transition, the threads reaching backwards or forwards through the years, depending on the starting point. When I became aware of her first, she had begun to drift through the spaces of her life, no longer believing perhaps in the aspirations of her younger self, or in the value of putting the best side out. I suppose the change was gradual, like the light fading and receding into dusk, but when you're close to someone you don't really notice. I think in the end she'd have preferred a kind of invisibility.

On Tuesday, when I found her portrait, I saw what she was like in the beginning. Maybe that explains the suddenness of my decision to leave, the lack of forethought. And now the image of the woman in Nassau Street playing on the screen of my mind, confidently displaying her fashionable clothes, her lines of bracelets, her garish eyeshadow, demanding attention. Confirming what I suspected about the futility of compromise.

I'm walking on Nassau Street again, feeling mildly foolish for scanning the crowds as if some kind of synchronicity might present her figure to me one more time. There are lots of people hurrying or strolling or standing outside buildings smoking, young people in groups laughing and chatting. I feel part of them, part of this, as if the city is one living breathing organic being and we are all just cells going about our business. The Dublin Theatre Festival is on. Earlier a poster in a shop window caught my attention, something about a circus, and I thought why not. I could use some distraction. I imagine clowns and cream pies and impossible situations. I like contradictions after all.

The venue is a little theatre in the grounds of Trinity College. The stage is in the centre like in a real circus and for a moment I worry that they'll expect us to participate. But it's ok. The clown in the barrel is just having fun, hitting balls at the audience which they must return, and everyone is enjoying the diversion as people take their seats. A good device to facilitate the transition from the world outside to the mood of the story they will create. The action is played out in mime, all exaggerated movements and elaborate gestures. There are only four actors.

Early on there's a shooting and then a ghostly presence in the form of the dead character playing the piano from a stage high up to the left. Most of the action centres on two men working out their rope act. They swing down from a platform, balance each other. An air of danger is created, a sense of drama and poetry as at key moments red petals are released from up high and float down along the trajectory of the rope. Tension is introduced, and longing, as a pretty young girl appears and is trained to balance with one of the characters. And then the archetypal story of jealousy and retribution presents itself. Two men vying for the attentions of one girl, her choice played out in the movement and height and tension and the danger of sliding and balancing on a rope high over our heads. We know that the chosen one must die, we all know it; but until the very last we hold out some illogical hope for another ending, a way to resolve the impossible. The sense of danger and drama is heightened as the beloved balances precariously on the rope high above our heads.

Then he's spinning on the rope, spinning in a wide arc, faster and faster, and the rope jerks, and the man begins to fall in lurching movements. But I do not see him anymore; I see the red feathers falling, I see the portrait of my aunt, I see the image of the woman on Nassau Street. I adjust the image so that the woman has no face, and the thread that connected all the pictures of my aunt snaps and everything floats away with the petals. Nothing remains but the image of my aunt in the portrait I hold onto and then there's the dead thud of a body hitting the floor.

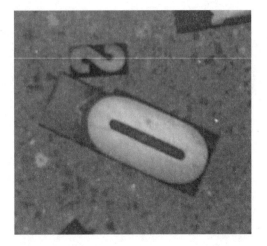

Neville Keery

Neville Keery is a Dubliner. His writing career includes a spell in journalism, a term in the Irish Senate, many years in Brussels with the European Commission, some documentary film scripts, and two collections of poetry (1999 and 2007) and he is a reader at the Chapters And Verse Lunchtime Readings. He is now engaged in a memoir project, *Surprised by the Years*, which reflects on his "three-score years and ten", 1939 to 2009. The following is the first publication of the draft chapter for 1941.

1941

The first holiday trip I can remember in clear Technicolor was when I went with my mother, her sister, Auntie Gwen, and their long-standing friend Lillian, whom I would call "Auntie Lillian" throughout her life, to Courtown, Co. Wexford.

Courtown was a small, popular holiday resort on Ireland's sheltered South-East coast, served then by the steam trains linking Dublin to the port of Rosslare, further south.

Rail travel was a real joy and adventure for small boys. There were signal boxes and water towers with dripping hoses at any sizeable station and turntables at major stopping points like Bray, Co. Wicklow. The passenger carriages were split into narrow compartments with a door at each side opening directly onto platform or track. Passengers could only open the doors from the inside by lowering the window so that they could lean out and turn the heavy outside handle. The windows were manipulated with heavy leather straps, like those used to make harness or to strop cut-throat razors. Punched holes in these straps allowed travellers to open the window for ventilation. Parents with children always had to wrestle with the dilemma of hoisting up their infants so that they could feel the rush of air and smell the steam as the train moved off or of refusing any such adventure on the ground that you would get smuts in your eyes, or your clothes covered in soot, as the big locomotives strained to gather pace.

Gorey was the station for Courtown and my first holiday memory is of being frightened by black shapes wriggling on a patch of grass between the platform and signal box. My fear subsided when, brought down the platform, I could see and understand that the black shapes were the glistening heads of calves protruding from the mouths of the sacks into which they had been tied so that they could travel more easily in the train's guard's van.

(In describing the calves now, I appreciate how troublesome the images must have been. Many worries and fears last until one can find a focus and context which explains what one is seeing. Great artists replicate the mysteries of "seeing" and "understanding". I think of how frightened I was of the dream sequence in Bergman's *Wild Strawberries*, the first "art" film I went to in the little Astor Cinema on Dublin's Eden Quay.)

Getting from Gorey to Courtown meant a trip in a pony and trap. My stock image of such transport is an amalgam of cheerful driver or jarvey flicking a tall whip, with a plaid rug tucking in passengers and luggage, to give them what seemed a false sense of security. Traps and side-cars always seemed precarious as they jerked along road surfaces that were often little more than skiddy gravel. An exception, on future holidays, would be the stylish landau-type carriages lined up outside Bray station to transport visitors to the hotels on the promenade.

Courtown accommodation was boarding house rather than hotel and there was no sense of promenade. My other memories of that holiday are very specific and are of colour and style.

Getting dressed involved putting on a little Viyella suit, the colourful check of the short trousers buttoned directly on to the matching check shirt with patterned metal buttons. I am uncertain about the comfort but remember being admired.

I seem to remember beans, but to be honest am not clear whether it was my first experience of being offered baked beans or "Smarties", the little chocolate sweets covered in a hard icing which spilled out from a cardboard tube in a multitude of colours. Orangey-pink is the colour I see. Was that the colour of the Viyella, of the baked beans, or of my favourite Smartie?

On the Courtown beach, as I sifted the sand with my fingers, I discovered lots of little snail shells, yellow, brown, grey, and some also orangey-pink. I definitely remember Auntie Lillian hanging such shells on the branches of twigs which could be stuck in the sand to stand up like miniature trees. "Prune trees", she said.

Sometimes on the beach there was talk of hearing the crump of bombing and even seeing the flash of anti-aircraft fire. I can vaguely remember thunder-like rumbling. It could easily have been thunder. The interest to the adults was that the noise might be bombs falling on Liverpool, not far across the Irish Sea. I was a baby in a world at war

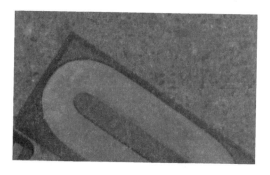

Noel King

Noel King was born and still lives in Tralee. His poems, haiku, short stories, reviews and articles have been published in over thirty countries. His debut collection *Prophesying the Past* will be published by Salmon in 2010.

The Letter

I hold a letter my Grandfather wrote;
the daughter of a woman he wrote to
found it packed in an attic of things.

April 3rd, 1947, Castlegregory, County Kerry –
he didn't live there, was on holiday,
his wife, my uncles and mother

probably cavorted on the sea-shore –
as he scribbled in secret
to this woman he kept from everyone,

probably saw only a few times a year
when his company called their conferences,
AGMs, branch managers' meetings and things

at the H.Q. in Dublin city, where he might have
rented a room for her to come to him
after finishing work in her Civil Service job:

pretending to the landlady she was his wife.
They might have dined and danced
and made love all night, perhaps not, I don't know;

all I know is the tickles of skin upon skin
and scribbles of dark blue ink
have – years after his death – found him out.

It might have been all innocent
and they slept alone, an intelligent-like-minds
thing, but the letter has great passion,

he calls her *my love* – while Granny slept
by him and cooked and cleaned
for him and reared his children with him.

The letter says he's packed a salmon,
caught with his own hands, ice packed it
and the runner-boy at the factory he runs

put it on the train. He wishes she could fish
beside him some day, maybe some day...
expresses shock that the Russians

were blocking Ireland's entry to the UN
because of de Valera's war-time
sympathy with the Axis Powers

and Franco's Spain. He hopes
the landlady at her digs has recovered,
would not after all have to sell up

letting her tenants of that many
years off to find new places to live.
The woman's daughter and I

plan to meet, muse upon the secret,
wonder why more letters don't exist.
Maybe his love destroyed them near her end,

that it broke her heart to burn them all
and missed this one. I'm not telling
my wife, anyone, that I am having this

meeting in Dublin, will share the secret
of her tryst with my Grandad,
take it to my own grave.

Lynne Knight

Lynne Knight is the author of four full-length collections, the most recent of which is *Again*, published by Sixteen Rivers Press in 2009. *Dissolving Borders* won a Quarterly Review of Literature prize in 1996; *The Book of Common Betrayals* won the Dorothy Brunsman Award from Bear Star Press in 2002; and *Night in the Shape of a Mirror* was published by David Robert Books in 2006. She has also published three prize-winning chapbooks, *Deer in Berkeley* (Sow's Ear Press), *Life as Weather* (Two Rivers Review), and *Defying the Flat Surface* (The Ledge Press). A cycle of poems on Impressionist winter paintings, *Snow Effects*, appeared from Small Poetry Press as part of its Select Poets Series and has been translated into French by Nicole Courtet. Lynne lives in Berkeley, California.

Safe

My first doctor skied through the night
into Sweden. By day, he hid in the forest,
sleeping in the hollow of a fallen tree,

in the shadows of a copse, and then as night
pulled its wide cloak through the trees
and over him, he strapped on his skis

to follow paths thrown down by the moon.
I knew none of this when he held me,
weighed me, peered in my ears and throat.

He was dead before my mother began
the story of his flight, the new words
Jew, Nazi, war. And the border he crossed

without knowing, realizing it only later
when he came to a sign on a road—
the border meant all he had left behind,

my mother said, and shook her head
before she spoke of the house, the lace
curtains his mother made, their border

of baby roses. It never occurred to us to ask
how she knew all this, how she could tell
the bitterest root he ate, the black walnut

he cracked a front tooth on while he stood
on the road, reading the sign, breathing
hard, like my sister and me in our beds.

Song for the Coming Winter
for Jerry and Geri

In an abandoned orchard—*Quince,*
he says, *what do you do with quince*
besides make jam?—Look at the blossoms,
one of the women says while the other
stares down at light in the creek bed,
light on the bright moss climbing trunks
of oaks and poplars along its edge—
he shows them the sleeping hut
high on the hill, barely used now
that the neighbor has poured so much
concrete into the view, and they cross back
over the covered bridge he built that cost
a hundred poems, maybe, nothing like
the ten thousand poems he spent building
the cabinets in the living room where,
come winter, he intends to do nothing—
Nothing, his wife repeats, happy
at the thought of all the quiet—
while poems fall out of the sky, tumble
down branches and trunks, over bridges,
out of cabinets right into his hands.

Quincy R Lehr

Quincy Lehr is a native of Oklahoma, recently returned to New York City after an extended stint living in Ireland. His work has appeared in numerous journals internationally, including *The Barefoot Muse, Cadenza, Crannog, The Dark Horse, Decanto, Iambs & Trochees, Measure,* and *The Shit Creek Review.* His first full-length collection, *Across the Grid of Streets*, was published by Seven Towers in 2007. Quincy is Associate Editor of *The Raintown Review.*

Sceneshifts

I

Just past the Georgian buildings, as I near
the traffic-choked bridge, I listen to the noises
that burble like bubbles rising from the river,
stagnant and stinking. Not exactly feared,
those unwashed memories, although I shiver—
and blame the cold. The sounds of far-off voices,
slightly familiar, whisper parts of phrases
that I should recognise, as unseen gazes
rake my hair—or is that just the wind?
Why do I think of you, and do I stutter
as I cross the bridge and reach its end,
breath uneven, pulse a nervous flutter?

City of absences! I tried to hold
the memory like fading rays of sun
that glisten in puddles, shifting to reflections
of headlights as the sun sets. It gets cold.
Disoriented by random interjections,
I speed up till I'm nearly at a run
and almost home in streets devoid of you,
with strangers passing and a constricted view
of steeples and a river and the stars
suffusing through city lights to reach the ground,
offset by the sound of soft guitars
filling my head with wistful wisps of sound.

Lay me down to sleep, if I can rest,
O Lady of My Memory and spread
the sheets above me, covering my face,
until the heartbeat throbbing in my chest
diminishes, and wisps of dreams erase
my thoughts. Unsure if I'm asleep or dead,
and heedless of the consequences, I
will stay here, motionless, beneath a sky
both starless and unseen, a canopy
of stucco framing this, my mute repose,
and you, O Lady of My Memory,
will lie beside me as my eyelids close.

II

A shift of scene. Move forward from one stop
onto another as it's getting brighter.
The bus pulls in, and I almost drop
my cigarette while fumbling with my lighter.

'Were you the man who used to sing the songs
out on the square
for change or bags of weed
as passers-by would pause to yell requests
in other native languages—
love songs, dance songs, the news of the day?'

And silence
as memories returned that weren't mine
but anecdotes of someone else's travel,
thumb to the road, a foreign subway line,
a threadbare coat just starting to unravel.
'Jhoo are Eenglish yes?' The look goes blank.
'You've got the wrong guy.' Pause. 'Oh, you're the *Yank.*'

Which one are you? Which woman's absent shoulder
won't support my head as I wake up wincing
and stare out the window, ever so slightly older,
memories more jumbled and unconvincing?

But the practicalities...
Did I remember to pay the parking meter,
keep my vowels up front, pronounce my R's,
lock the door, shut off the stove and heater,
and cast my lot against the distant stars,
savouring the morning's cautious glow,
overdressed for as-yet-distant snow?

And a series of busses
and tourists chatting in my native tongue,
and I thought, *Dear God, have I been gone so long?*
as I shared in the distaste
for the ignorance of the timetables
and the denominations of the local currency,

and I stared
at the expanses of new estates
miles away from the anecdotes
of ageing buskers.

The memories are running far away,
a squeal of tape rewinding, back to shops
stocked full of sweets, the sky a bluish grey
above an empty rugby pitch, then stops,
and for the merest fraction of a second,
a half of an iota of an instant,
I can feel her head against my shoulder,
remember fondling locks of curly hair...
and know that this is much too much to bear.

Did we break even?
Did we make out like bandits?
No, more like clumsy, eager adolescents
groping in cars, a quick ejaculation,
and crises on the family vacation.

We wondered if we still could make it back
on what was in the tank, and held on tight,
a love of necessity, a shocking lack
of exit plans within the incipient night.
And in the press of half-formed recollections,
tickets in pockets, and noisy interjections
from passengers debating their directions,
the scene shifts further as a brooding dawn
glowers above the trees, and we move on.

III

Rain. And the river, wrathful, surges
unheeded in the headiness of a half-dream night.
The living lurch in layers of the skull,
and I rise retching, wracked with the sense
of a meeting missed, a marred assignation.
Is fever at fault? The foul weather
whips past the walls, but the wind mutters,
O Muse of Memory, mother of the restless,
who delves in dreams, digging for samples

in stab-marks of stars or the stutters of phrases
I couldn't quite acquire for my tongue.

And you, who lie asleep beside the water,
alone, in company, dead drunk or sober.
riding high, incipiently hungover,
someone's lover, someone else's daughter—
guarding the gold that rests in the riverbed
even if its gleam is false. Unseen,
it can't be turned to numbers, but instead
can only shine.

                    I don't know where it's been,
what bold adventurers have sallied forth
from Hyperborean strongholds in the North
to seize it, or what gouty Nibelung
whispered nothings through his half-held breath
(not much to look at, surely, but well-hung).
But each scenario's been done to death.
Watch over me, maiden, as I drift to sleep,
and sing your arias in gentler keys,
voices like a river, flowing deep.
Alto clef, not brazen Valkyries.

IV
But here, a dashed-off note, and here, the wreck
that rises to the surface for a second,
propelled into view by violent turbulence
I cannot see. The remnants of the deck
rise at an angle.

                    But no mermaids beckoned;
someone else's filched inheritance
came to nothing. I watched from far away
as if the mess were none of my concern,
as if it were footage filmed some other day.
Type it up, then save and press Return.

Old e-mails on the screen,
and sentences no longer meant return
in pallid cyberlight, the time between
shrunk to an instant; embers start to burn.

And I must have reread those words
at least a hundred times
as the rain fell in bitch-slaps on the roof
and the frozen pizza turned brown in the oven with
                              the temperature set too high,
and two drunks on the street staggered by singing
                              'The Fields of Athenry'
as they stuffed their faces with lukewarm chips,
and a teenaged girl, young and beautiful and aching with the
fatal joy of being human,
pressed her middle finger to the window of the Subway shop.
Forget her
          and do better.
                              I'd forgotten
everything, except for random jetsam
that mingled in the surf, bleached out and rotten,
items that haunt you... *only if you let them.*
But I remembered, far too well, a place
no longer mine, a different port of call,
and botched itineraries, and a face
that launched some ships.
                              It wasn't that way at all.

V

Midnight; wan electric bulbs resume
their vigil over stacks of crumpled paper,
dirty dishes, an ashtray's unkempt bloom...
and memories of the way her fingers taper...

That weekend night, the music blared, its bass line
                              thick.
I took a corner spot,
watched nubile rear-ends shaking to a Latin beat,
and ordered up a shot
then got another beer that cost me far too much.
I didn't dance at all.
I wondered if I still looked suave—or still looked thin
while sitting by the wall.
Those evenings end. They rarely go the way you'd like.
The morning doesn't care
about the disks the hipster deejay spun that night
or whether you were there.

They just let go when weekdays are too much to stand.
They buy another round
and lose themselves in dance and draughts of alcohol
and gushing throbs of sound.
Why can't they goddamn see the well-lit exit sign,
the reasons to mistrust
the dead end of the sensual, the awkward blink
that frames that gaze of lust?

Paracetamol. A drink of water.
A bad kebab, a wince through one last smoke.
The heat's set where it was, though it seems hotter.
I don't know why, but it's the perfect joke...

I didn't see the city much that languid week.
I barely went outside.
her head by mine, a single, narrow pillow shared,
the gratitude and pride
that she was sleeping next to me... it still seems
                                    strange,
like someone else's life,
or maybe like a thin and arid fantasy
of someone else's wife.

It's just another round you never mean
to drink, and then you find yourself outdoors,
dew on the ground—a slick and chilly sheen—
then street, then locks, familiar corridors...

Now no one's hands but mine will rearrange the sheets
in night-time tugs of war.
There's no one here to grumble at my coarser ways
or grimace at my snore,
and in the short term, I will lie awake in bed
and murmur to my pride
that this is just another stage of life, and that
I'm glad she left my side.

And heedless of the consequences, I
will stay here, motionless, beneath a sky
both starless and unseen, a canopy
of stucco framing this, my mute repose,
and you, O Lady of My Memory,
will lie beside me as my eyelids close.

Éamonn Lynskey

Éamonn has had poems published in many magazines. He was nominated for the Sunday Tribune/Hennessy Literary Award for New Irish Poetry in 2006 and one of his poems featured on the 2009 OXFAM calendar. His first collection Dispatches and Recollections was published in 1998 and 1. His second collection *And Suddenly the Sun Again* will be published in 2010. Éamonn, who holds a Diploma in Italian Language and Culture has also translated the works of modern Italian poets into English. He is also a long time contributor to the open mic scene in Dublin.

OMIGOD! Not Another Newgrange Poem
with some indications as to delivery 'a la mode'

(*Please strike a pose consonant with
the dignity of the lines you are about to deliver*)
It is an ancient law enacted by
Aosdana that every Irish Poet be moved
to write about Newgrange once every year
for competitions, or to be declaimed
to multitudes in a monotonous poetry voice
(*like this*) while standing in the pouring rain

beside the ruins. Said poets should write, nay, sing
about the silence of her ancient stones,
the roundness of her ancient stones, the hardness
of her ancient stones, the ancientness
of her ancient stones, the stoniness of her ancient
stones. And how it is they yearly speak
to us (*No, no! Read that again, and this time
lift the voice on 'us'*) ... And how they yearly

speak to us across millenniums, nay,
millennia (*Pause. Significant pause,
look up, stare at the audience, look down. Sigh*).
And how the solstice penetrates her passage
yearly on the front page of 'The Irish Times'.
And how the nation yearly feels the need
to re-discover prehistoric roots.
Or prehistoric Truths. Or. Booth.

And how the Nation casts its gaze back
to those ancient days (*more feeling!*) ...
to those ancient days when men were men
and ate their meat raw, sucked the bones,
and dressed in off-the-shoulder furs, went clubbing
for their women, and had a deep relationship with stones and knew the stars and how
to roll enormous rocks on poles (small 'p')

up from the Boyne Valley. Knew to carve
involved and complicated rings and loops
with their ancient tools, and knew the Mystery
of Life Itself, (*pause*) and how to chart
the sun (*look up and pause again*) to make it
strike along this passageway. Today
it can be done at any-old-tourist-time
thanks to the Board of Works installed a light

to creep along the floor when it's switched on
like this: (*!) Excuse me, sir, but could you move
your foot a little... Thank you. (Bloody tourists!)
Now behold! (*step back and gesture towards
the floor*) The Sacred Light that lit the dark
before old Moses was a boy in britches!
See (*step back again and mind your head*)
The Sacred, Sacred Light that every year

attracts ten thousand weighty poems, replete
with abstruse references to the Druids, each poem
ten thousand times the weight, and more, of
                              Newgrange,
and all her ancient stones. (*!)... Mind your heads
on the way out and please don't help yourselves
to free souvenirs. It costs a fortune to replace
these old stones with new ones every year.
And there's a bucket for tips at the entrance.
Don't fall over it.

It's That Man Again!!!

And at last it's feet up in the evening,
now for a beer, a spot of TV, and—
don't I deserve it, after getting through
another daily dose of bullshit and bellyaching—
now for a bit of personal time, a bit
of ME-time, a splash of the goggle-box—
OH NO! It can't be! IT'S THAT MAN AGAIN!!!
JESUS CHRIST!— No, I don't mean 'Jesus Christ'.
I mean: JESUS CHRIST! IT'S THAT MAN AGAIN!!!
saluting, waving, embracing crowds— Just where
the hell would TV be without him?! Well,
the so-called 'History Channels' anyway,
and nothing much in the documentary slots
on all the rest but 'Anniversary Programmes'
they put on to make good goddamn sure

we don't let sleeping Japanese or Germans
lie for long in case they might forget
what evil, nasty buggers they were once
until WE straightened them out with Hiroshima
Nagasaki, Dresden. And never a night
allowed to pass but HE is wheeled out, and
especially when the television schedules
aren't tight, or when they're fresh out of fodder
for the gaping multitudes (of which,
yes, I am one). I'm sitting there, deciding
whether or not to take my socks off or
get up and fetch another can of beer and—
There he is! IT'S THAT MAN AGAIN!!!
IT'S HIM AGAIN! Addressing crowds again,
gesticulating, ranting, grimacing—

or being nice and playing with his dog.
And where the hell is the remote?— But no!
There's no escaping him! He's everywhere!
On BBC he's masterminding ruin
for everyone he doesn't deem quite 'kosher'.
On Channel 4 he's spreading out his maps.
On UTV— No use. He's out to flatten
Russia on a level with her steppes,

his *einsatzgruppen* singing lustily
the *Deutschland uber Alles...* Yet— And yet
it always ends the very same, though only
after endless frames of speckled footage
and the lengthy reminiscences
of gnarled faces telling how he could
be charming. Yes, it always ends the same,

in spite of all the crowds, the motorcades,
the sycophantic henchmen, all the hands
uplifted in that straight salute— It always
ends the same with that great aerial shot
of the Reichstag burning and I think (socks
off by now) thank God he's gone for one night.
Must be snooker on somewhere— Let's see
the TV Guide?— A spot of football, maybe?
Where's those Girls of Playboy Mansion? But
NO! It can't be! IT'S THAT MAN AGAIN
JESUS CHRIST! No, I don't mean 'Jesus Christ'.
I mean: JESUS CHRIST, IT'S THAT MAN AGAIN!!!—
It's HIM!— But wait!— It's only part of him!
They've found a bit skull in a paper bag
on a shelf in some old dusty war-archive
somewhere in downtown central Moscow. And—
They've made a programme out of it, with lots
of that old footage seen a thousand times
before, plus coloured bits they've made themselves
stuck in to liven up the show. Cue
gnarled faces, same as seen before
(It's true! Old soldiers never die! Especially
those who talk in Russian with subtitles).
Then an expert in white coat comes on
and tells at length that if you open up
a box and find a bit of someone's head
you can be fairly sure they're fairly dead.
At last, I think. He's dead at last. And now,
that beer. And now those 'Desperate Housewives'.
But no! Another sciency chap comes on

and starts to question whether or not that bit
of skull is part of THAT MAN'S skull. It might be.
Then again, it just might not... And now
I'm on my knees and pleading with the screen.—
Have mercy. Please let him be finished off.
Just for tonight?! One night! A single night
without the Reich was built to last ten million
television documentaries!
Relentlessly the sciency chap goes on
and on and on and then there's shots of labs
and microscopes and then the screen fills up
with stuff they say was never seen before
and then— IT'S THAT MAN AGAIN!!! Yes,
IT'S HIM AGAIN!!! The trench coat. Peaky hat.
The toothbrush 'tash. The staring eyes. I'm sorry,

I just can't go on...

****

When Gravediggers Die

(in memory of Thomas Scanlan and Denis MacNamara, of Crusheen,
Co. Clare, d. July 1987 R. I. P.)

The two old men who dug the graves
for all who died around Crusheen
these years and years last week themselves
took to the clay. They, who times

more oftener than other men
had heard the ragged shovel-shot
methodically subtract one other slot
from out the gravelled earth—

They who leaned so nonchalant
along the boundary wall, then mixed
unbidden in among the mourners, joined
the decade, then became all

on a sudden all transformed,
their shovels setting them apart,
their heave and heft mechanically
detaching them from us. When

gravediggers die, there must come
a tremor in the crust of time whereby
the world of stones and trees takes pause:
leaves stop sighing, whitened gable-ends

fixate the sun in stasis
momentarily - when nettles
cease their close embrace of headstones,
all uncertain. They who stayed

behind to flatten out the mound
and then to stake the haft, spit
on their palms, push back their caps
their pipe-smoke trailing incense upwards,

casually surveying all their handiwork
around them— When gravediggers die,
we know the world has shifted in its orbit.
They whose spades these many years

have mapped the limits of our lives
must now themselves stare upwards as the earth
collapses downwards, blotting out
the sun. And we ... We ...

When gravediggers die, we
feel the loss of lore, the eye
that navigated more than other men
our wide galactic oceans of decay.

(First published in 'The Burren Meitheal' 1995, and subsequently in
the collection *Dispatches & Recollections,* Lapwing 1998)

Hugh McFadden

Hugh McFadden is an Irish poet, literary editor and freelance journalist. He was born in Derry, lived briefly there and in County Donegal, before moving to Dublin. There he was educated at the Synge Street CBS and at UCD, where he studied English, History and Political Science for his BA degree. He earned an MA degree in Modern History at UCD and was a Tutor in the History Department there in the 1960s and early 1970s. Later, he was a Tutor in Politics at UCD and a Lecturer in Journalism at the DIT and he worked for many years as a journalist with the *Irish Press* Group of newspapers.

Blues in the Afternoon
(i.m. Shay McGonagle)

Dear Shay,
My good friend John Jordan used to say:
'some of my best friends are dead'.
I know now how he felt then.

You left us without saying goodbye:
and, after so many years in show
business, as you called it,
no obituary was written
and no news item marked your passing _
not even a line drawing.

Do you remember (of course you do)
that old Woody Guthrie song
'So long, it's been good to know you',
well, that was more or less how I felt _
that, and the feeling you used to get
when a bluesman with soul sang the blues,
Sonny Terry and Brownie McGhee
say, on this *Sporting Life Blues*.

Wish I could sing it for you:
but, where you have gone, you don't need it.

'So long, it's been good to know yuh
So long, it's been good to know yuh
So long, it's been good to know yuh,
This dusty old dust's getting' mah home
And I've got to be driftin' along.

Mise en scène on the Street

(i.m. Ronnie Drew)

When Sackville Street
was ransacked by
local scumbags
or gurriers _
(native villains
red white and blue
Jackeens, untrue Dubs) _
who stuffed their sacks
and bags with loot
and scarpered down
O'Connell Street ...

Where Big Jim Larkin _
fiery agitator,
would-be liberator
(after the great-cloaked Dan
with his wounded angels) _
raised aloft his arms
in supplication ...

get up off your knees
stand on your own feet

And the long-lost Chief,
Charles Stewart Parnell,
at the Rotunda,
pointing his finger
at the hospital
where the women lie-in ...
no man has the right
to fix the boundary
of a nation

Near this same scene,
within gunshot,
stood Pádraig Pearse
reading aloud
the Proclamation

(at the very spot
where all the postmen
filled their bulging sacks)
proudly intoning
those famous words ...

Irishmen and
Irishwomen:
In the name of God
and of the dead...

Where James Connolly
marched to the GPO
from Liberty Hall
and raised the Starry Plough ...

The worker is the slave
of the capitalist
society, the
female worker is
the slave of that slave

Only a stone's throw
away in space-time
WB Yeats
stood and declared:

you have disgraced
yourselves again

And, again in
Sixty-six, shots
rang out sharply on
rooftops once looked down
on by stony-faced
Admiral Nelson

(it's not beautiful,
said Senator Yeats,
grey brick upon brick,
wrote Louis McNeice) ...

Nelson's Pillar _
rude reminder
of the power
of an empire,
its former glory,
and Horatio
Nelson's victory
at Trafalgar ...

kiss me, Hardy

Nelson's Pillar _
Joyce's omphalos
phallic standing stone,
a naval navel,
Anna Livia's
tight belly-button
right in the centre
of the hunting ground _
pricking a summit,
a peak on a plinth,
a towering spire
piercing the lowering
Hibernian womb ...

ripe pears, apples and
 juicy oranges

Round the corner
stood Jasser Joyce,
leaning on his stick
at the heart of his
own metropolis,
paring his nails
while the ould wans,
all the shawlies,
hawked their fruity wares

apples and oranges
and ripe juicy pears

Then *The Dubliners,*
in their effrontery
and high drollery,
sang out their ballad:

But one-thirty in
the morning, without
a bit of warning,
Nelson took a powdher
and he blew: oh poor
old Admiral Nelson
toora-loo

They're nearly all
gone, now, to their
eternal rest.

Orla Martin

Born in Donegal but having spent her formative years in Galway, Orla Martin graduated with a B.A. Degree in English and French from the National University of Ireland Galway. A. Currently based in Dublin, she works in the Financial Services Sector. Publications include N.U.I.G. magazine *Alpha '89, Cuirt Poetry Journal '98*, the women's' anthology of poetry *Jumping the Bus Queue 2001* and the *Cathal Bui 2001* anthology of poetry, *The Cuirt annual 2003, The Scriobh Poetry Anthology 2006* and *The Stony Thursday book* (no 5). She has read as part of Poetry Ireland Introductions Series. Her poetry has been highly commended at the South Tipperary Festival of Writing '98, the Clogh Poetry Festival 2000 and Francis Ledwidge Poetry Award 2007 and also 2004 and Short-listed at Scriobh Poetry competition 2004. The poem *Paddy* won the Cathal Bui Poetry Competition in 2002. Her work has been published in *A Page in the Life* collection by RTE from The Marian Finucane Show and broadcast on The Sunday Show and also The Marian Finucane Show. Founder of Muse Writers' Group in 2006, Orla runs an Open Mic in The Winding Stair bookshop in Dublin and has been a guest speaker at Ra at the Cobblestone, Patrick Kavanagh Celebration, Carnival open mic, Monster Truck performance space and Last Wednesday Reading and Open Mic.

Hola

He calls from B. A.,
        leaves a message on the phone,
                in my hall.

Hail outside, door agape
        I stand, drops down my neck
                phone in hand.

Hear the words from his mouth, his afternoon
                gentle heat, mosquito buzz
                        on the line

and the hall fills with rain, cascades down,
        thunder cracks, I am drenched.
                        Message saved.

****

Stranding

Came to grief,
flensed of flesh,
mottled grey
armour torn.

Winter bleached,
blubber worn.
Just carcass,
just bones

suspended.

Rachel Metcalfe

Rachel Metcalfe is nine years old. She lives in Stamullen in Co. Meath and when she was eight she wrote this poem for a competition at her school St Patrick's National School, Stamullen, for which she won second prize.

When I Am Old

When I am old
Will I dance and sing?
Will I have a wedding ring?
Will I have a glasses?
Will I have false teeth?
Will I even play outside on the street?
Will my friends be here?
Will my friends be there?
Will my friends be anywhere?
Will i have any pets at all?
Will I even play basketball?

Dónal Moloney

Dónal Moloney is a writer and translator from Waterford. The excerpt published here is a version of Chapter 4 of a novella called *In the Balance*, which he is currently completing. An alternative short story version of Chapter 1 of the novella received a commendation in the 2009 Seán Ó Faoláin Short Story Competition. An excerpt from his short story *The Mask* appeared in *Census: The First Seven Towers Anthology*. He is a regular featured reader at the Chapters and Verse Lunchtime readings and the Last Wednesday Series Reading and Open Mic events.

In The Balance
Chapter 4

Brian stands sweating in the cramped, hot 'small room' while Marie runs round the house looking for her mother. Marie is a bright student who has been making good progress in her French. But on this sunny evening she spent most of the hour looking wistfully out at the boys and girls sitting around on the green outside. When the hour was up she bolted out of the room to get the money to pay him.

He checks his watch again. He has plenty of time to get to Jonathan and Helen's house – last week he even fit a sprint round the supermarket in – but he's still agitated. He follows the footfalls upstairs. What's taking her so long? Has she even found her mother yet? *Come on now, Marie, will you, please. If I was a taxi, the meter'd be running.* He yanks his mobile out of his shirt pocket and switches it on. He stares at the screen for a minute before locking the phone and putting it back in his pocket. Finally there's the sound of fleet thuds on the stairs, and Marie bursts in with an apologetic look and two fistfuls of shrapnel.

Brian leaves and starts winding his way through the neighbourhood. He looks idly at the little front gardens as he passes. Of those not converted into drives, about one in two are tended. 'On top of life, not on top' he repeats to the rhythm of 'She loves me, she loves me not'. His own patches, front and back, haven't been weeded since the previous summer and are fairly ragged. A group of kids ahead are having a water balloon fight in the last of the daylight. He crosses the street and keeps a nervous eye out for stray missiles.

His thoughts snake back round to McEvoy's mention of Mad Ludwig a few hours before. This was the students' nickname for Cathal Greene, the school's other history teacher. Were McEvoy and Deegan getting grinds off Greene behind his back? Surely Greene would have cleared it with him before taking students of his on. Besides, if he had been giving them grinds, he would have sorted out their special topics. (Here the image comes to him of Greene reading the essays and indulgently smiling at Brian's negligent correction work, giving a beatific little shake of the head.) No, McEvoy and Deegan were probably just comparing him unfavourably to Greene. Or had he heard them right? It might have been insecurity suggesting a name that hadn't been spoken at all. Maybe, even, they were talking about the historical Ludwig II of Bavaria.

From time to time, Brian wonders how Greene ended up with such a cool nickname. Greene was ten years his senior and a legend in the school. His reputation as an inspirational teacher was matched only by the science teacher John Callaghan's. Greene's students consistently got better marks than Brian's. He also suspected clued-in students of rejigging their timetables at the start of fifth year to make sure they got Greene. Greene was very popular in the staff room too, especially among female teachers. 'A proper man' was how Mary O'Sullivan the Irish teacher had once described him to Brian, a remark he stewed over for days, sniffing an implicit rebuke to him in it. In his mind he addressed questions to her like 'Why for the love of...would you say that to me? What do you know about men, you freak?' and, after a good stew, 'How can I possibly know what you mean by that without knowing your entire history of relationships with men?'

He is jolted from his brooding about Greene by a scrabble of feet on pebbles and explosion of barking. He flinches, raising his arms. This must look comical, because he hears children break into laughter. It is only a terrier behind a locked gate. He looks round but can't see the children, though they are still laughing. He glowers at the dog, his heart pounding. But the dog just bares more of its teeth and growls deeper. 'Bark all you want behind that gate, you mutt. You come out here, you'll get some kick in the snout,' Brian growls back before walking on. He notices he is carrying his mobile in his hand. He doesn't remember taking it out of his pocket. He studies it for missed calls or messages even though it is set to vibrate and the tones are loud. It's three minutes to eight. Seriously though, Mad Ludwig! And what does *he* get for a nickname? Bandy Legs.

Arriving at Jonathan and Helen's street, he stops and leans against the waist-high wall surrounding the garden of the corner house, having checked first for a dog. He opens the Drafts folder on his mobile and reads the message stored there: *Hi Helen, it's Brian here, hope you don't mind me contacting you by text. I won't be able to make the grind today. I'm in bed with an upset stomach. Very sorry. See you and Jonathan next week.* It had taken him an hour to compose in the study hall earlier. He had then spent a further fifteen minutes dithering over whether to send it. And though his thumb had hovered over and even grazed the Send button, he didn't press it. So here he was with the same decision to make, only later and ruder if he cancelled now.

So, just go ahead and do the grind, Brian. You've walked over here. It's the only decent thing to do. At the start of every year, you stand before rows and rows of new faces and get on with teaching them. Just walk up to the house, ring the doorbell, go in and give your best. Move now.

Unconvinced, his feet stay still.

But why not ring her? Give yourself another week. Say you're in A&E, banged your head, a bit of concussion, nothing serious, you'll see them next week. It's only a minute past, it's not too late. A quick call and it's done.

He scrolls down his address book to her name, then stops and groans. The problem is that he can't imagine himself being any stronger the following week. He is also afraid that his treacherous intonation would rasp "Big dirty lie!" against the grain of his words. And then he would have to listen to Helen's response and hear, even if she pretended on the surface to buy the excuse, all the irony and contempt in her voice. Who was it during his childhood that had said to him, 'You're just a little shit, aren't you?' And he knew he had deserved it and had no answer. But a child moves on from this quickly, whereas an adult's dignity abjectly crumples under the blast of a merited insult.

A car slows to take the corner where he's fretting. He looks down at his feet, scared of seeing Helen's penetrating eyes narrow as she leans across to peer out the passenger window. And it is fear, ultimately, that is stopping him entering that house.

Fear of him sitting at the round table with the sky-blue tablecloth and the doilies, two shut doors at his back between him and escape, Jonathan bearing over him across the table, declaiming a string of weighty, justified recriminations, reason and measure in his voice, him unable to understand a word.

Helen there too, having decided to sit in on the grind, her weary eyes burning with disgust, her puss acidly indicating that she knows well he doesn't understand what Jonathan is saying; him waiting for her to translate; her holding out; though not out of cruelty, more a resoluteness to let justice take its true, untampered course; him not really needing a translator all the same, knowing what Jonathan is accusing him of: greedily taking on too much work and not doing right by any of his students; being a lousy teacher, never having had a vocation for it, only choosing it out of expedience; once having fetishized the idea of being a teacher, but not having the stamina, the *heart* to be a good one.

Jonathan leaning forward and back over the table according to the rhythm of his rhetoric, then – in the grip of an especially strong denunciation – leaning right forward and Brian being confronted close up with the massively wide gape of his raw, swollen mouth; Brian's personality – silent until then but still busy behind the scenes in observation, judgement – shutting down like an electrical appliance in a blackout.

Fear of Jonathan accusing him further of being on the side of the bad, those who go all funny when they see his face, who have hurt him all his life, from babysitters to plumbers. *But mightn't I reasonably have expected more from a teacher, all the same?*

Something catching the light between them, from under Brian's chin: his crucifix, which must have popped out over his shirt; him seeing the reflection off it glint in Helen's eyes; Jonathan still speaking, accusing him of insincerity, of having come back to religion with a lot of big ideas in his head, but without substance to his faith, of talking big about God and wanting to feel it, but with a faith so unestablished that it is rocked by a deformed face; him knowing that Jonathan is asking 'Is God the artist of this face?' though he is unable to hear the nuances in Jonathan's voice or read the expression on his face, even Jonathan's eyes nothing other than interrogation to him; him unsure if Jonathan is upbraiding him for not being able to believe in God the artist of his face, or for previously having believed in God the artist of all things only for his face to trigger a crisis of doubt. *My face! How dare you let my face throw you into a crisis when all I wanted from you is your French.*

Him sitting there dumb, reviewing the charges as they pass; the charges being true and fair to differing degrees, with mitigating factors; but him unable to respond to them because in his heart of hearts he knows he is *absolutely* guilty; contesting individual points being like taking part in a massacre and then correctly pleading that you only bludgeoned five defenceless people to death, not six.

Fear of Helen and Jonathan falling on him with knives and taking out a lifetime of various disappointments on someone who was guilty; not guilty of it all, or even of much of it, but *definitely* guilty, guilty and there; fear of crossing their threshold and – in that very second – being hostage to their mercy.

Fear even of the accusation expiring from Jonathan to be replaced by a softer, purer interrogation, willing Brian to look at him, listen carefully to him, engage with him; the look that was there in the beginning but which he had failed in responding to; a frightening failure, of a different kind to the other hurtful failures of his life: costing his under-11 football team the league in the crunch fixture with a nightmare back pass with his bad leg; screwing up his Leaving Cert exams and getting marks well below what he had been getting all year; not finding anyone for the Debs; a failure different and terrifying because it was fundamental, like getting a poor one-time-only grade from God in Overall Worth; or – with him as Belshazzar, Helen as Daniel and the face of Jonathan as God's arcane script – like being told you have been weighed in the balance and found wanting.

Joe Moran

Joe is a sculptor and artist from East Wall in Dublin, where he still lives. Among his public art works is The Family Group sculpture in Fairview Park in Dublin. Joe is a full member of the Temple Bar Gallery Studios.

No Change

A play in one act

Characters

Narrator: elderly man

Girl: young girl in her early twenties plain and unkempt

Young Man: thin, dishevelled and self assured

Setting

Man's bedroom in guest house

Time
Early morning

Summary

This play is about how people's lives go on. It is about how they don't change, they go on doing the same things they go running watch TV do the same thing every day, life never changes, monotonous boring.

ACT I: Takes place in bedroom
(Man in bed. He lifts himself up in the bed to look at the clock)

Narrator: Six, the same as yesterday it never changes but I think it will change today. I'll get out of the other side of the bed today.
(He lies there thinking)

Narrator: But that wouldn't be a change. Change is something that just happens not when you know it's going to happen. If I get out the other side of the bed today I would have to walk around for me slippers, for they would be on the other side. No, I'll do it tomorrow. I wonder what time it is. I think I better get up.
(He pulls himself up on his arms, swings his feet out of the bed, puts his feet into his slippers which are more worn and thread bare so much so that his feet are more out of the slippers that he is in them)

Narrator: I must get a new pair of slippers someday (he pauses, looks down) I'm not going to a dance they'll do me for now. I think I'll have to take this nightshirt off. Now what would I do that for sure there's no one comin to see me. I'd only have to put it back on tonight.
(He goes to the door takes down and over coat which looks as if it is too big for him it's made from a dark tweed-type of material. He rubs his hands down it as if to make sure it fits him. He pulls it around him tightly and then lets it go to hang loose he turns looks at the table which has one chair. He walks slowly to the chair fixes it moves it stands back and looks at it fixes it again once more again he walks around and looks at it like somebody who is looking at a painting making sure that everything is right. Only when he is sure that it is in the right place does he sit down ever so slowly as if he was at a child's party waiting for someone to pull the chair from under him. He sits waiting for the girl to come with his breakfast as she has done for all the years he has lived in this guesthouse. He knows what she will say when she comes in; he goes over it in his mind.)

Narrator: I heard you moving about I knew you would be hungry so I brought you up a nice bowl of porridge and some toast. The porridge is good for you, good for the inners. You're looking good today, sleep well? Course ye did, when you're finished just knock down and I'll come and take it away from you. Eat it all up now.
(Still looking into space he gets up from the table slowly moves back the chair looks at it to make sure that it is in the right place. He walks to the window, rubs it with the sleeve of his coat and looks out)

Narrator: (low whisper) No change just as it was yesterday.
(He walks around the room touching the wallpaper as he goes. He comes to the fireplace where the mirror hangs with the clock in it he stares at it.)

Narrator: (even lower whisper) Now, six always six I must get it fixed someday
(He hears a sound on the stairs he turns and goes to the table more quickly. He sits down at the table then as he does a girl comes in, carrying a tray, plain looking young girl hair looks as if it has not been combed. The black skirt she is wearing is too tight for her it is now turning white. As she walks her feet are thrown out as her shoes are worn down on the outside. She starts to speak as she puts down the tray not stopping at all...all in one breath)

Girl: I heard you moving about I knew you would be hungry so I brought you up a nice bowl of porridge and some toast. The porridge

is good for you, good for the inners. You're looking good today, sleep well? Of course you did, when you're finished just knock down and I'll come and take it away from you. Eat it all up now.
(Turns and walks to the door not looking back says)

Girl: Bye now.
(He has not said a word just keeps looking at the tray on the table. Now places his hands each side on the tray on the table (pauses) then he slowly takes the cloth that covers the tray he starts to eat his porridge as he does he begins to think)

Narrator: I think I'll sit on the other side of the table today
(As he is facing the window his face lights up at this thought)

Narrator: but if I was on the other side of the table *(Pauses and questions himself)* if something flew by I wouldn't see it but that never happens.
(Lifting the bowl up in his two hands he scoops the porridge into his mouth as if he was afraid that someone was going to steal it from him)

Narrator: *(out of breath)* that's finished left not a scrap.
(Looking quite happy with himself, he is like a man who has achieved a great goal in his life.)

Narrator: I get up in the morning and go to bed at night. I will have to change, tell you what I'll sit on the other side of the table. I will I'll do it.

(He looks happy but excited twisting his hands he looks at the tray with the bowl and a small plate with toast on it and a mug of coffee. He leans forward as if he was pushing a large heavy weight. Slowly he pushes the tray as if he was waiting for someone to push it back only when he is happy that it is on the other side does he get up. Again slowly and he takes the chair with him puts the chair down stands back and looks at it to make sure it's in the right place where he wants it stands back again shifts it a little)

Narrator: that's right.
(Only then does he gently sit down like a man who has a back problem)

Narrator: *(happy)* there I have changed. I knew I was going to do something different today. I don't care if something does go by the window. I knew I could do it.
(He looks at the toast picks one piece up)

Narrator: Only toasted on one side.   *(He turns it over and over)*

Narrator: still only toasted on one side maybe it's to save time they do that.
(He pauses looks around looks up at the ceiling now he is questioning himself)

Narrator: what do they do with time when they don't toast both sides of the bread? Do they put it in the bank and take it out when they get old. Or do they leave it to somebody *(pause) (wondering look)* No, time is like the wind it comes and goes, it never comes back. My mother said she'd be back when she took me to the big house and left me there she said I can remember her as if it was yesterday she said I'll bring your home you'll only be here for a little while. I was there until I was sixteen. She said these are nice people they will take good care of you for these are God's people. You will make lots of new friends for there are boys here your age. She kissed me and gave me a small teddy she had just bought for me. She walked out of the door of the room never looking back. I never seen her again she never came back to take me away from this place of endless nights of horror.
(He begins to shake his head and his hands more frequently now he pauses, looks up at the ceiling)

Narrator: I must stop thinking of these things.
             (He looks at the toast eats some of it)

Narrator: I'll keep one for later.
(He tries to put it in his pocket but just cannot he pushes and shoves but it won't go in. He looks around shaking his head)

Narrator: What to do? What'll I do with this piece of toast? I'll put it under the mattress. *(He gets up and slowly walks to the bed, lifts up the mattress and as he does pieces slowly fall out. With some effort he gets them all back under he now looks happy once more)*

Narrator: That's better.

(He walks slowly back to the table and now he is on the opposite side to where the chair is. He stands looking at the chair on the other side. Once more he begins shaking his head and his hands from side to side a couple of times, thinking that somebody has done this change. Somebody has changed the chair to the other side without him knowing it. He slowly gets up and walks around the table to where the chair is now he sits down ever more slowly than before. He looks around to see

if there is somebody in the room with him. He looks to his right to see the clock but now the clock is on his left)

Narrator: *(excited)* where is the clock? No clock, the door is where the clock used to be and the window is gone.
> *(He pulled the coat ever more tightly around him)*

Narrator: Who change this? (Pause) I made the change.
> *(He stops shaking he looks happier)*

Narrator: yes I did. I don't like this side.

(He takes the chair walks around slowly, places the chair stands back, looks at it to make sure that it is in the right place. Shifts it a couple of times one last look before sitting down slowly on the chair. Pulls the tray back over to where he is sitting. Pulls at it as if someone was trying to pull it back from him. Everything is where it was before, the clock in on his right and the window is in front of him so he feels happy, now picks up the mug of coffee.)

Narrator: I don't like coffee I told her that before (pause) that would be a change if I sent it back. Oh! No. I sent the apple back once I never got another one. I'll drink the coffee.

(He drinks the coffee and eats the last piece of toast. He then proceeds to brush himself down brushing the crumbs out of the beard he has.)
Narrator: Now all that's done. What to do now?
> *(Sits looking into space)*

Narrator: I'll go for a walk.
(He walks slowly to the window and just as before he rubs it with the sleeve of his coat, looks out.)

Narrator: No change.
(He turns and walks around the room examining the wallpaper as if he has never seen it before, comes to the clock.)

Narrator: Six, still six.
(Looks at it as if it has changed slowly he walks back the same way to the window rubs it looks out.)

Narrator: Yes, no change.
(He walks back to the table sits down as before. A look of happiness comes over him. He picks up the coffee mug and places it down then he picks it up once more and places it back on the tray. Then he shifts it a couple of times to get it back in the right place. That makes him

happy. Sitting in the chair rocking backwards and forwards looking into space he stops. Puts his hand on his head then to the table and pauses pushes up slowly and moves the chair back then replaces it. It he walks to the window rubs it with the sleeve of his coat then as before he looks out)

Narrator: *(low whisper)* No change.

(As if there was someone else in the room with him. He walks around the room examining the wallpaper rubbing it in the same place. Seeing it for the first time he notices that this place has no flowers on it for this is because he has been rubbing it so many times over the years. He stops and looks its changed he gets excited his head and his hands begin to shake.)

Narrator: Who did that? How did it happen?
(He moves slowly looking backwards and forwards moving back to the fireplace as he looks at the clock he stops shaking.)

Narrator: Six, no change.
(But this time he doesn't go back the same way it leaves him looking at a blank wall)

Narrator: Where's the window?
(He looks left and right more quickly than before. He starts to shake nervously he doesn't know what to do for this was a change he wasn't thinking of. He stands confused shaking)

Narrator: What did I do wrong?
(He looks at the wall where the window should be. He looks at the floor. He looks at the wall again, walls left and right of him)

Narrator: Something is wrong, I must go back.
(He turns slowly, then he sees the clock. Now the shaking stops.)

Narrator: *(loudly)* Six, no change
(He quickly walks to it like someone who has just met a long lost friend. He stops and looks at it for a while. Then and only when he is satisfied that the clock has not changed does he walk to the window rub it, look out, he looks happy. Places so gently on the floor like a man who is walking on ice. Then he comes to the table gently sits down slowly like a man with haemorrhoids.)

Narrator: Now that's better the window is still there. How did I get to the other side I must think (pause) I knew I would do a change today I just knew it. But one must be in control of change, for change without control is no good. Even for those who are changed by it. I don't like change. I'm finished.

(He knocks down by stamping on the floor. As he does he looks at the floor for some time like someone examining a rare painting)

Narrator: I don't have to change anymore today. Change can become a way of life if it's not stopped (pause)
                    (Rocking his head backwards and forwards)

Narrator: I don't like change. I always get hurt when there's change. I'm still hurting from the time I was in the big house from what the man of God did to me that night.
                    (His hands now begin to shake)

Narrator: He would say it won't hurt. But it did hurt. It always hurt. I've never forgot the hurt
(He looks like he is in a trance, eyes wide open staring at the ceiling head shaking up and down . Suddenly there is a sound at the door. Awakes him from his trance and man enters. he is youngish. Black trousers white shirt sleeves rolled up he walks kinda slowly as if he has something wrong with his hip)

Young Man: Finished squire? Of course you are.
                    (Never letting him speak)

Young Man: I can see that now.
(He just sits there looking at the man waiting for every word to be spoken. The man is all the time taking up the tray never looking at him)

Young Man: It's going to rain today I can always tell from
                    my Rheumo it acts up.
(Now he begins to get upset, for the man has never say that before)

Young Man: It's not good for me to come up these stairs
                    when I'm like this with the Rheumo.
(Never looks back at him. Finishes cleaning up the table walks turns and goes towards the door never looking back just walking on. Says without turning...)

Young Man: Have a nice day
                    (.......goes out the door.)

Old man looks more nervous than before. He stands up and down looking around several times

Narrator: He's never said that before what's going to happen to me?

He gets up from the table shaking his head and his hand goes to the window rubs it looks out

Narrator: Nothing's changed
He looks a little longer than before now the shaking slows down he walks back to the corner examining the wallpaper rubbing it. A smile comes to his face.

Narrator: Narrator: No change.
(He turns to the clock, that has not changed he comes back to the table and sits down slowly. He turns his head from side to side)

Narrator: the window is still the door si still there there the clock is there what can be changing there must be change why did he say have a nice day? I don't like when people say have a nice day when I worked in the bank they used to say that to me.

(Breaking some toast from his pocket and crunching it)

Narrator: I remember when change came at the bank we were not to be called Mr's. anymore but by our first names. They started calling me Joe not Mr. Murphy. Even boys who just came into the place called me Joe. Me! There for thirty years. I opened the bank up in the morning and made sure the kettle was on for those who came in. That was me up at seven washed and shaved. They would say you could set your clock by me. He never changes they would say. Every night I went for me walk hail rain or snow, in bed after the ten o' clock news. I spent my two weeks in Galway the same house every year. Two weeks in September. I met the same people. Then it changed new owners they never gave me the same room as I had before even when I told them how long I'd been coming and getting the room. I like that room I said I'm comfortable in that. No I couldn't have it they said, it was given to somebody else. The one they gave me I couldn't sleep in it the door was in the wrong place and the wall paper I didn't like it and the bed was in the corner not the corner it was in before I had to get up to look out the window. no I just didn't like all that change so I stopped going. that's why I like it in here no one changes a thing here. *(looks around the room)*

Narrator: If I like to I could go out I'll do it now.
(Gets looks at the door up slowly goes to the door stands back a little)

Narrator: I will I'll do it that would be a big change I'll
          do it.

(He puts his hand out slowly as if it is being pulled back by something he doesn't touch the door he looks at it. once more he stands and stares at the door like a man in endless space)

Narrator: why do I want to go out? I will only have to go come back in to go to bed. I'll go out it tomorrow.
(He turns and goes back to the table looks at the chair, moves it a little turns it moves it a little sits down slowly looks from left to right twisting his hands.)

Narrator: why did he say have a nice day? I will see if anything has changed
(He gets up from the table walks slowly not making a sound as if someone was sleeping in the room and he did not want to wake them he walks to the window cleans it as before, looks out)

Narrator: No change.
     (Walking, rubbing the wall paper as he goes examining it)

Narrator: That's good, no change.
(To the clock in the centre of the mirror he looks as if he is expecting it to change he pauses)

Narrator: No change.
(He walks back the way he had come. Cleaning the window once more looking out he stands back shaking his head in approval)

Narrator: No change.

(Walks back to the chair moves it stands back looks at it to make sure it's in the right place when he is satisfied sits down slowly puts his hands on the table looks at the door...)

Narrator: Tomorrow I know I will have to change. I once had control over change but they took it away from me (Pauses) I must become the master of my life once more. I'll do it tomorrow.
     (He gets up from the table and goes back to bed.)

Anne Morgan

Anne was born in London and grew up in Dublin. She studied English at St. Patrick's college, Maynooth. Anne has done readings in the Ballymun Axis Theatre and the Irish Writers Centre and has had work published in *Newsfour*, *Riposte* and *Electric Acorn*.

Lights in Blacksod

This is where they fish,
old boats
bobbing on the water.

I remember meeting
old Mr Sweeney
Or Ted as he was known.
He was the keeper
and master of the sea.

This historical place
Where men were lost
The lighthouse stands sentry.

Shining its light
over the bay,
welcoming the survivors.

Helena Mulkerns

Helena Mulkerns is a writer, journalist and photographer. She was born in Dublin, but has lived elsewhere for much of her life. In Paris, she began writing freelance for a variety of publications, and continued to do so after moving to the U.S. in the late eighties. She has written for *Hot Press, The Irish Times, Rolling Stone, Music Express, Downtown Magazine, Elle, New York Perspectives, The Irish Voice, The Irish Echo, Irish America, Film Ireland, Cineaste, Irish Tatler, The Sunday Tribune* etc. etc. She has also contributed to two non-fiction books, *The Irish In America*, and *Motherland* and was live New York presenter on the popular prime-time Irish television series, *Gerry Ryan Live*. Her fiction has been published in the *Sunday Tribune* newspaper and in collections such as *Ireland in Exile* (Ireland), *Wee Girls* (Australia), and *Cabbage and Bones* (U.S.) *Shenanigans*; in Penguin UK's alternative travel anthology *Fortune Hotel*; in the Random House anthology *Thicker Than Water* and in *Turbulence - Corrib Voices* (see more below). Her short fiction has been nominated twice for America's Pushcart Prize, and she continues to publish short stories regularly in magazines and newspapers. In 2008 she won an Arts Council Bursary for her current work in progress.

The Biggest Liar in the World

Lime-green digits flickered down the massive black screen suspended over the Departures Hall. London, Dubai, Paris, Istanbul, Dublin - okay. The disembodied woman's voice directing him to Gate 82 for flight LH 179 confused him, but eventually he located the gate number he needed on the screen and headed off, under the terminal's glassy dome, towards the distant departure gate.

He was beyond tired at this point, only half there, in Frankfurt, and the rest of him somewhere on the South Sudan border. There was something about the old man's eyes that he couldn't clear out of his head. Here he was a day away from the camp, thousands of miles from it, trying to psyche himself into holiday mood. Yet random images kept flooding into his consciousness: the shrill, unnerving throng of excited children that followed them around the camp, the lines and lines of barefoot women and old men queuing up for barrels of water.

He'd been travelling now for more than thirty hours. MI8 chopper from the refugee camp to the border base; a military transport plane from there to the capital – a change of clothes and suitcase grabbed before the 747 to Cairo, where he changed for Frankfurt – and now, he was on the last lap home.

He walked down a sloping corridor, and an air hostess at the boarding gate flashed him a *cailín deas* smile, and he revived somewhat until he was arranged gratefully into his window seat, and then dozed off again.

Behind his closed his eyes, the shimmering spectacle of Wadi Dun Camp swam into his brain. His first refugee camp. Eighteen thousand human souls in various stages of malnutrition, dispossession and despair. *Refugee camp.* Two simple words read a thousand times, heard on the news since childhood. But no amount of repetition could ever have quite made him understand what they actually meant, until he spent two days walking around one.

A swill of sour Egyptian coffee played fisticuffs in his gut with a block of gluten formerly known as bland German toast; he declined the cailín's offer of weak, metallic tea. He never felt so less like eating, or so wretched about feeling sorry for himself. After all, he was just tired, plonked in a calm, air-conditioned environment, in full health, with a home to go to and a sound pair of shoes that kept out the scorpions and the broken glass. He was on a safe aircraft that smelled reasonably pleasant that had a real seat and no groaning Medevac cases in it. The toilet worked. The blue and teal scrolls that made up the pattern on the seat in front of him looked luxurious, extravagant. Something so pretty for such a functional purpose.

He looked around at the other passengers. The Bulgarian grandfather looking out the window to his left reminded him again of the old man deep in the heart of Wadi Dun's smelly, winding laneways. He needed sleep. It would be nice to see Ciara. Maybe.

The air hostess woke him to straighten up his seat as they were coming into land. Glancing sleepily out the window, expecting the dusty brown swathe of a desert landing strip, he was momentarily startled. Peering through the rain, a sodden gray-greenness was visible on each side of the runway. He was briefly overcome with a wave of something indefinable, what? Possibly sheer relief. Simple gratitude that it was still there, still wet and grey – home.

His sister stood just beyond the barrier, new boyfriend in tow. Kev. In finance. Or that's Finance, to you, mate. Way-too fancy glasses for a straight man, but a solid Northside accent that somewhat redeemed him to Bren. Ciara was effusive, charged with her usual Celtic Tiger verve.

"So great to see you ... brilliant ... are you starving? I have a full Irish all ready. But look at the state of you, poor muppet. You're wrecked! You're in bits!"

"I'm grand."

"Look, we'll just stop in at Valumart on the way home, and then you can jump into bed, I have the new spare room made up for you. It's totally IKEA, you'll be really cosy."

"Great."

The motorway that came at him swiftly through the grey tinted windows of Ciara's SUV removed any sensation of home that had affected him during the landing. The grass banks and generic signs could be on outskirts round New Jersey or Barcelona; how fast Ireland was catching up with the rest of the developed world's mediocrity. Ciara was talking about the new house, and her kids, and other stuff he wasn't really taking in.

"And what about yourself, anyway? Things going well? .... Bren?"

He jumped, realizing she'd just addressed him directly.

"Em, yeah ... "

"Well, we're all dying to hear what you've been up to over there. Later anyway, when you've had a rest?"

"Sure."

He smiled at her, and lay back against the seat again. At a traffic light, Ciara watched him in the rear view mirror with some concern. His eyes were closing and opening, beyond his control, apparently. He didn't look well. His e-mails were always upbeat, full of the wonders of Africa and the work he was doing in the capital of that place – she could never remember the correct name of it - just finished one of its wars. Maybe he was just travel weary. She veered left off the motorway and, after a perfect curve, into the mammoth compound of Valumart.

"You stay here, Bren, we won't be a minute ..."

Headquarters had left Wadi Dun camp until the last stop on the visit, to show the inspection party from Geneva how it had degenerated since its emergency construction three years previously. How it now needed a massive new influx of funds. Very fast. Not two words easily associated with Geneva.

Little images kept repeating themselves in his head: one child running ahead of him with lacerated feet, still smiling and laughing with the others. Kids playing on the jagged metal remains of a jeep. A beautiful little girl, peering painfully at him through an eye-infection so bad she could hardly see – but also smiling. Beside a laneway, half dust and half furrowed mud, a young teenager standing with one foot in a stream of foul waste as it made its merry way. Bren was lagging behind the HQ team now, didn't feel up to their banter, in awe of the way the camp dwellers who had adapted to this unbelievable environment.

In front of the dwellings – mostly tents – people were living their ordinary lives, washing clothes, weaving baskets, making furniture. The flaps of the canvas were held down with ragged rope and the roofs were overthrown with large blue plastic tarpaulins, slung over and tied down on each side. It looked like a set from Mad Max – some of the hovels were almost organic in their form, constructed with wattles and refuse. Others were straightforward United World issue, beige canvas, sullied with red dust and rotted after several rainy seasons.

A woman in her fifties, working away at a wicker basket, shot him a blinding smile and nodded her head. Her beautifully plaited hair framed an emaciated face. He smiled back. Behind her, an old man was standing, trying to adjust the ropes of his tent. He was also emaciated, and it looked like the severe frown over his eyes had been burnt on by the sun. As he caught Bren's eye, he motioned for Bren to approach the tent. When he went over, the man slowly showed its material to him, worn thin, fraying at the edges. His big, hooded brown eyes gazed at Bren sadly, as he tried to knot together two pieces of rope that formed part of the vital tarpaulin-roof.

"Look, he seemed to be saying. Look at this piece of shit tent I have to house my grand-children in – it's falling apart."

The gnarled hand was filthy with days-old muck, it looked like. Bones distorted. He must suffer horribly with the arthritis in the damp of the rains: As Bren felt the rotting cord, a kind of sandy powder fell through his fingers; some of the threads were just breaking away from the main skein of the rope. The rest of it probably wouldn't last another month. Certainly not for the deluge of the monsoon storms.

"I'm sorry," Bren offered in useless English. "I'll see if I can get you some better rope." Rich. How would he even remember where this old guy's tent was from among the thousands of dwellings, even seconds later, as he continued up the camp? The old man nodded again, leaning his head to one side, never taking his eyes off Bren.

"I promise. I'll try and find some new rope for you for you."

From way up ahead, someone called his name. The inspection party was out of sight now. Maybe he could bring them back down to show them this. There was nothing more to say, and the old man shook Bren's hand solemnly before he took off down the laneway.

He hurried up the slope to where the others were piled into the jeep now, impatient. They were discussing large-scale use of displaced populations as human shields by the Government in the capital, of which Wadi Dun was an example. He couldn't get a word in edgeways. After two days on the border, everybody was hoping to make the last flight of the week back to the capital. The connecting choppers didn't wait around on the outpost runways. As the small convoy pulled off, kids were tearing after the white jeep, squealing and pushing, as it drove towards the main gates. Already, the location of old man's tent was lost to him. He felt like the biggest liar in the world.

He thought he would join Ciara and Kev inside the supermarket, since his head was spinning and he needed to walk a bit. Opening the door, he breathed in the cool damp of the North Dublin air with an unprecedented appreciation. His feet felt strangely pampered as they alighted on the smooth surface of the car park. It was new, perfectly finished, marked with gleaming white lines like a slick piece of abstract art. The even bitumen was unexpected beneath his feet, along with the lack of a smell in the air.

Walking up to the store's entrance, it struck him that there hadn't really been a public smell in his nostrils since he had got off the plane. The richness of an African marketplace, with the sacks full of spices, the donkey shit, the heat and cigarettes - and the arguing scent of fruits rotting and fresh all at once, seemed stronger even in his memory, than the polished plastic tiles on the floor of Valumart.

He stood inside the doorway, gazing up at the high, vaulted ceiling, and then from side to side, where the walls of the place had two football pitches' worth of space between them. It was like one of the huge World Nutrition Organisation food supply hangars that lay down the road from the tiny airport in Odalia's capital, almost bigger than the airport itself.

No, it was like a cathedral, its arched ceilings towering over the shoppers, as they traipsed reverently around the aisles, performing the ritual of choice.   Choice – that was it. He looked around. Filling the waist-high troughs for metres and metres to his right was the most astonishing selection of fresh vegetables and herbs.

"Wow." He was suddenly animated. "Basil. And Coriander!"

"Yeah, so?" Kev had spotted him from the organic counter.

"Mushrooms!   ... and avocado ... And look at the *broccoli* jesus ... "

"Are you taking the piss, Bren?" Ciara coasted up behind them, amused..

"Can we buy some broccoli?"

"For breakfast?" Ciara snorted and grabbed some, then forged onward, trolley-filling.

"What, so there's no vegetables in Odalia then?" quipped Kev.

Bren thought about how to answer this. Simply: no, there are not very many vegetables in Odalia. More accurately, well, broccoli costs fifteen dollars a head in the capital's market place, and is only affordable to well-paid international workers. He decided to leave it out, wandering off, taking in images that his brain repeatedly balked at.

The word, perhaps, was *overwhelming*. Shelves and shelves of tins, packets, bags, sacks of stuff. Biscuits for dogs. Cat food. Pasta, beans, oatmeal, eggs, fish, poultry, cheese.   Plates, stools, cutlery, pots, pans.

A family could set up house in one of the tool sheds in the garden section and fill it abundantly with stuff from these very shelves. You could feed them for a month on the contents of a single giant freezer that lined one of the aisles.

He was stunned to observe the bank of shampoo products, sparkling in their pastel and day-glo ooziness.. They seemed to cater for all manner of hair requirements: greasy hair; frequent wash; dry scalp. Colour treated. Dandruff healing. Gel for styling. Extra volume. Manly ones in black and red packaging, girlie ones in pink and lilac. Shampoo in all fragrances, from mango to chocolate to mint and papaya to soothing sea salts for essential repair. He had forgotten that people had such a variety of preferences when it came to their hair.

Moving along, he counted nineteen different kinds of fruit juice. Smooth, with bits, without bits, fortified with calcium, Vitamin C, from concentrate, fresh and organic. The milk was more or less the same. Full-fat, low-fat, skimmed, goat's milk, soy milk, fortified and

UHT. He didn't know why this should bother him, except that he kept thinking of the little fabric and metal scales that hung from a dead tree branch in one corner of the camp, where that girl Gina had set up the weigh-station that determined which children (only the most redeemably undernourished) could qualify for powdered milk supplement. He thought of the steel pincers that measured the non-existent fat on the tiny baby arms.

Shit. He had to get real fast and lighten up, now he was home. He decided to find Ciara again. She'd sort him. But everywhere he turned, things appeared surreal, or hyper-real, or just maybe bloody unfair. Something ...

Ciara had left the fresh food produce now, and her trolley was wobbling with items that she thought might tempt Bren, whose main problem, she'd decided, was fairly drastic weight loss.

"Fancy anything there, Bren?"

Bren was flanked now on both sides by tall, cool white cabinets, filled with meat, fish, pies, croquettes, pizzas, egg rolls, onion bagis, shepherds' pies, garden peas, mushy peas, marrowfat peas, any kind of fucking peas you liked.

"They have nineteen different kinds of fruit juice. *Nineteen.*"

"Hm. And this is your nineteenth nervous breakdown, apparently!" she smiled, but he didn't smile back. "Cheer up, Brendan, what's wrong with you?"

"Ah, he's just happy to be back in the real world, that's all," Kev chirped. "We'd better get yah home, Bren, before you lose your marbles altogether."

Bren turned around, thinking just to head off out of the company of these two jokers, and was confronted by too many people, swilling around the aisles of the supermarket. It was almost, in its weird way, like the feeling he had two days before in Wadi Dun: there was no end to the people, crammed into the market-like laneways in the camp, where there was no end to the shacks, the dilapidated canvas shelters, the snot-nosed, impossibly innocent children, the winding passage ways, the sun assaulting his eyes, the smell of unwashed misery; the despair of old men.

It was in the space between the bargain South African wines display and the checkout registers that Ciara found herself in the embarrassing position of watching her ragged little brother fall to his knees under the fluorescent light of the food department, and set to weeping like a baby. Or not really. He was weeping in a terrible, muted kind of way. His face sort of fell into one of his hands, while in the other he clutched, inexplicably, a twist of gaudy orange-coloured nylon chord, the kind used for cheap washing lines. What an earth did he think he was doing with that.   She observed him for a few seconds, in bewilderment.

Punters lined up to purchase their weekly bargains stared unabashedly, glad of the distraction. Ciara had never seen grown man weeping, not that she had never even thought of Bren as a grown man before. And yet, there he was, twenty-eight years old, crumpled into an ungainly pile of grief.   For one second, she was almost overcome herself.

"What's wrong, Bren, what's wrong with you? What is it?"
Bren didn't answer.
"Are you alright? Are you sick?"
"No, I'm fuckin well."
"What is it then?"
"You can get everything here ..."

Ciara didn't really understand why that should be a problem, it was the reason she'd chosen Valumart in the first place. She put her hand awkwardly on her brother's shoulder, in attempted consolation.

"We can go home now, if you like, okay?"
"There's ... so much stuff ..."
"Look, why don't you take the car keys, and we'll finish up paying here, we'll be out in a few minutes, okay?"

Bren took the keys of the SUV from Kev and walked slowly outside to the vehicle, his eyes burning, head thumping now. He jumped violently when the body-less synthetic voice over the exit doors thanked him for shopping at Valumart, and then continued out into the car park, clutching the nylon clothesline tightly in his hand.

Rick Mullin

Rick Mullin is a journalist, painter and poet from New Jersey. Rick's work has been widely published in journals, including *The Raintown Review, Measure, Envoi, Unsplendid, 14 by 14* and *The Chimera.* Rick's book length work *Huncke* will be published by Seven Towers in 2010.

Amity After the Fire

My muse returned from war. Her swollen stumps
were wrapped in rags and paper as she pumped
her arms and pushed her yellow skateboard down
the sidewalk. Amity is back in town
and living in my basement now. I hear
her castors on the floor at night—I'm near
exhaustion, with my inspiration stuck
for benefits despite her service. Luck

would have it, sleep is not among her needs.
There's constant feeding, though, and when she bleeds—
it happens intermittently—my heart
contracts and ices up. I have to start
compression on the remnant of her thigh.
She gently stokes my hair, and then a sigh
I never heard in all her teasing days
accompanies an unfamiliar gaze

from eyes that used to tell me something strange.
They've lost their mystery. As I arrange
a knee-high desk for Amity, prepare
myself to take dictation, I'm awares
he's crossed a line. I used to chase her form,
those perfect thighs, her arms and hair would storm
into my life and leave me nights of sweet
fulfillment or frustration. God, her feet,

the perpetrators of the vixen's trick
of disappearing for a week...A stick,
now, and that slab on wheels. I couldn't touch
her then, yet here I dress her wounds. So much
has changed since Amity embedded with
the wind, "Before the Fire!" her shibboleth.
It echoes in my soul—the soul that longed
to lie with Amity, the soul so wronged

and yet rewarded. Now, I want to sleep.
But I'm on call, her needs are dire, and deep
into the night my ministrations plait
a prelude to the work that she claims fate
prefigures. "Canto I," her voice, without
its old élan, surprises through a bout
of smoker's cough. "A cold two minute warning—
cerulean engines. Sunlight. Tuesday Morning."

•••••••••

John Paul I
For Michelle Brunetti

I can't retrieve the temporary pontiff's
face beyond that pink filet of haunted
newsprint in a miter. Substantive.
Formidable, but blank within a gilt
display. Torn out, the image was (what killed
him?), from the Sunday magazine. The milk

of Christ's beneficence kept burbling on
his smock, and draped upon the paragon
was lingerie! The pope was dead and gone
in just a month and a memorial
came cobbled to my dormitory. All
irreverence and mock theatricals,

sophomoric sculpture with the plastic flowers
from the coffee table—gothic horrors.
Mary Wollstonecraft would keep the hours,
it seemed, in leotard and black brassiere.
The dance of Salome in veils was there
where Strickland crammed biology. His sneer

betrayed him. Prophylactic irony
prevailed, a filter on the Holy See.
That famous smile does not come back to me
and thus I tend to substitute my father's
heavy features—"Wait! That holy water's
for the plastic flowers!" Sons and daughters

frolic in the dormitory lobby
and, to tell the truth, we're kind of sorry
that a namesake and successor, holy
Karol, is in place. From what we saw,
a jagged smile across a Popeye's jaw,
there'd be no frills or flowers anymore.

Noel Ó Briain

Noel Ó Briain was born in Kerry, grew up in Dublin and now lives in Camolin, Wexford. He is a playwright and poet and a former head of drama at RTE. He has worked for many years in theatre, radio and television as an actor, producer/director, designer and script editor. He produced and directed many plays in the Damer Hall under the auspices of Gael Linn. He also designed the sets for many other productions. He won a National Jacob's Award for his production and adaptation of Seán Ó Tuama's Judas Iscariot agus a Bhean. His poetry and short stories have been published in a number of literary magazines including The Kilkenny Magazine and Poetry Ireland. They have also been broadcast on radio in the short story slot and on Sunday Miscellany. His first collection *Scattering Day, 21 Sonnets and Other Poems* was published by Seven Towers in 2007.

What Do You Think of Norma Jean?
(On seeing the iconic picture of Marilyn Monroe
reading James Joyse's *Ulysses*.)

What do you think of it Norma Jean?
Ulysses, I mean.
Is that a look of perplexity
Or the literary bloom
Of your sexity?
Can you make tail or head of it?
Or are you like the rest of us
Who only have read of it;
Or those who skip
To Molly's soliloquy
And eveasdrop on
Her sexability.

What do you think of it Norma Jean?
Ulysses, I mean.
Would James Joyce have been so keen
On Molly Bloom
If he had seen
You sashay across a room.
In Monroe mode as Marylin,
Your very shape
An occasion of sin.
With you sex never seemed sin-thetic
Like *Sex and the City.*
Norma Jean! I mean, *pathetic!*

What do you think of it Norma Jean?
Ulysses, I mean.
Is Stephen Dedalus just a bore?
Does Blazes Boylan
Make Molly a whore
As they cuckold old Leopold?
Have you read Homer's *Odyssey*
Or the tome of academics?
The key to codes of *parrallax*
Or *indeterminacy;*
Buzz words of
Joycean polemics?

What do you think of it Norma Jean?
Ulysses, I mean.
Child woman,
Who never would grow old;
Your life, no Odyssey.
- An Odyssey takes too long -
You sang a birthday song
To Mr. President;
Your swansong, Norma Jean.
On screen
The credits roll.

The End

****

A Poet May Know the Heart Undone

A poet may know the heart undone
As Yeats once knew
With Maude long gone;

And Dante as a boy did pine
For Beatrice though
She was but nine.

Yet neither of their muses fled.
Dante dreamt Amor
Held Beatrice in a cloak of red.

And Yeats, he drifted into myth,
Made songs of queens and warrior deeds
And swords hurled to the pit.

But in his heart still raged the storm.
Then peace came when
Time touched her form;

A peace, it seems, to end love's war;
For in his Celtic twilight years
He married George.

This is the road the poet may tread;
For you have been my Maude long gone,
My Beatrice wrapped in red.

Gréagóir Ó Dúill

Greagóir Ó Dúill was born in Dublin and grew up outside Belfast. He has published nine collections of poetry, two anthologies, a critical biography and a collection of short stories, and he has taken prizes in poetry, short fiction and criticism. He writes in both Irish and English and his w ork is widely anthologised and has been translated into the major European languages - most recently with a full-length collection of versions of his Irish poems in English by Bernie Kenny called *Gone to Earth*. He has read from Cork to Stornoway to Palermo to New York.His most recent publications are *New Room Windows*, (Doghouse, 2008), a collection in English, and *Dealbh Athar*, (Coisceim, 2009), a translation to Irish of Scottish Gaelic poetry by Christopher Whyte. In 2009 Gréagóir was poet in residence at the Princess Grace Library in Monaco. A collection of his work from that residency, *Gracenotes,* will be published by Seven Towers in 2010.

Place Names

I meet them at compass points at the end of a millennium,
not old men in snugs, foam on querulous moustache –

they'd all be dead by now. Each takes his place
where I, too, find myself, half by accident, not intending pilgrimage.

Pearse in Cullenswood, a wash of children surging in the corridors
of a Gaelscoil I took part in founding, his railroad logic laying steel,

Connolly in a chair (as at the end) in Pilot Street, child on his knee
became my father in law, talking up a strike to hard-faced men in caps,

Casement in Murlough on a boulder over Moyle, good boots well worn, his mind on
Belgium's Congo and the Amazon, diamonds and shackles,

Ledwidge bentbacked on the bridge at Slane breaks stone and rhythm, subverts Yeats,
listens to a noble call, enlists for little Belgium,

Plunkett walks to Magheraroarty, his stride pounds out a ballad
on the foot and mouth disease, t.b. be damned, wry romantic to the end,

McDonagh drafts some prose on prosody in U.C. D., not   bettered since,
Kettle takes up position in the Green, starshell clears his brain, his sight.

Ends and means, decisions and sacrifice and mere accident.
In camouflage pattern, deep eddies swirl in the estuary of time.

****

Last Resort

Heavy raindrops fall on shivering pools on the tarmac road,
ripple as ringmail links through the wetblack surcoat.

Wet clothes from my illjudged walk chafe my skin, rub it raw
as neoprened surfers hold their boards in front of them,
wait in dying troughs for the mythic big one.

The town is boarded up for winter, bar a pub
or two, the bay a dark pint glass frothing to a creamy head.
Estate agents' signs add spot colour to grey streets.

Churchyard tombstones moss a dying sect, its memorials
with blurred inscriptions of the khaki dead in France,
more recent cuts of those wore black a while, and
would have married them.

A drop runs down my spine, exotic, cold,
my shoes continue, disciplined, to move.

Crossing Over

A minor skill, but one which gave me pride and joy:
I moved fast and chancey on the rolling rock
Across small fords on rivers, beaches, estuaries.

Water runs fast, with gleaming highlights or foam
Streaks like smiling teeth.   From bank
To waiting bank I ran, foot rising as rock rolled

To glance against another and move on.   The weed,
Sargasso spread, that algal hair a threat
To trap me in flailing fall, ignominious slide
Into the freezing water with no change of clothes.

Speed slowed, bifocal lens a let-down, I no longer
Make fleet assessment of plane, angle and stability.
That joyful migration, one to other, is no longer fun.

I'll find a sunny spot out of the wind, lie flat,
Place my hat over my face, lie long, careful first
To mark the tide's advance and likely reach.

Fintan O'Higgins

Fintan O'Higgins is a Dublin based poet, playwright and screenwriter . He has worked as a script and story writer on various soap television soap operas and his plays have been produced in Dublin, London, Edinburgh and Leeds. His and poems and articles appear in publications in Ireland, the US, UK and Australia.

A Lesson in Civics
A play

There's a cash machine on the stage. Two men queue at it, and another sits beside the machine begging. The machine bleeps, the first man takes his money and leaves. The second man shuffles up, clearly nervous of the beggar.

The beggar himself moves uncomfortably. he presses a hand to his belly and extends his neck, trying to breathe normally. the other man backs away slightly. The beggar nearly vomits, manages to keep it down but finally throws up in a spectacular and revolting way, right at the other man's feet.

The standing man is disgusted and shocked. the other man, initially traumatised by his heaving paroxysms, calms and, after wiping his mouth and eyes, feels considerably better. The standing man continues to look at the beggar, however. the beggar can't ignore his gaze and sees that he has his eye on the puddle of vomit.

The vomiter looks away but the other man persists in his gaze. The vomiter sneaks a quick look back, but the other man remains looking from the beggar to the pile of vomit and back to the beggar again. at length, forced to acknowledge the other man, the beggar apologises.

Beggar: Excuse me. (*Beat*) I've been feeling a little under the weather.

ATM Man: And who's going to clean that up?

Beggar: The vomit?

ATM Man: You're practically sitting in it!

Beggar: Could be worse...

ATM Man: You've got some on my shoes, there's some on my shoes.
Beggar: Yes, be careful there. It's a bit of a mess.

ATM Man: Who's going to clean it up, I asked you?

Beggar: There'll be someone.

ATM Man: It's eleven o'clock in the morning. This disgusting pool of vomit is going to be stinking up this place all day. People have to stand here and get their money out. It's disgusting. Who vomits beside cash machines at eleven o'clock in the morning?

Beggar: I told you: I've been feeling a bit under the weather. A bit of sympathy mightn't be completely out of place...

ATM Man: How are you feeling now?

Beggar: Lot better, thanks.

ATM Man: Need some water?

Beggar: Nah, I'll be fine.

ATM Man: OK, then.

Beggar: Thanks.

Beat

ATM Man: So who's going to clean up this mess?

Beggar: You think I should do it? What makes you think that I should do it?

ATM Man: You're sitting in a pile of your own vomit.

Beggar: I'm not in it, I'm adjacent to it, and anyway I'm going in a minute.

ATM Man: And leave that there?

Beggar: I'm sorry, I haven't got bus fare for us both.

ATM Man: Wait...!

Beggar: Wait what? What? You really think I'm going to clean it up? Don't be disgusting. What on earth makes you think it's my job?

ATM Man: Then whose?

Beggar: The person whose job it is, that's who. (BEAT) I am currently between positions.

ATM Man: Please, just do the decent thing.

Beggar: What's decent about cleaning up a pool of vomit?

ATM Man: It's your vomit!

Beggar: How does that make it better?

ATM man steps away from the machine to talk to the beggar
ATM Man: Look – excuse me – if my dog, you know, fouls the footpath then I'm obliged to clean up after him.

Beggar: Well that's why I haven't got a dog... I mean they'll slobber on your hand and fetch you sticks, which might be appealing, but when all is said and done, they have you shuffling after them and clearing up their shit. They're laughing at you, citizen.

ATM Man: That's not the point.

Beggar: I know what the point is, and it's fallacious, so it is. For a start the rules of dog befoulment which apply in such public leisure amenities as come under the administration of the Parks Department and Office of Public Works do not apply to areas designated public highways. Secondly the practical concerns governing the so-called "scooping" of a more or less cohesive lump of dogshit are very different from those facing a flat pool like this one, dispersed over a large surface area. And with chunky bits.(BEAT) Haven't you got a job or something to go to?

ATM Man: Yes. You're right. I have. Bye, now.

Beggar: You haven't got your money!

ATM Man: I think I'll go to a machine that's a bit less vomity.

Beggar: Wait, but...

ATM Man: What?

Beggar: Obviously, I have a bit of dignity and that...

ATM Man: Obviously.

Beggar: But, you know, contrary to appearances may be deceptive, I do have some bit of civic conscience...

ATM man looks at him. The beggar is slightly abashed. Pause.

ATM Man: Are you asking me to pay you to clean up your own vomit?

Beggar: Suggesting. Since you feel so strongly about it... You do feel strongly about it, don't you? It's not as if you were just giving out to me because I happen to be a bit under the weather and – let's face it – undomiciled.

ATM Man: I wouldn't do that.

Beggar: I didn't think you would. You're a concerned citizen, aren't you?

ATM Man: And so should you be...

Beggar: Yes but my circumstances force me take a slightly more pragmatic view of things. To be honest with you, I'm pretty disenfranchised.

ATM Man: I already pay my taxes, you know...

Beggar: It's only eleven o'clock in the morning, though. That's going to be stinking there all day...

ATM Man: And you don't care...?

Beggar: Not that much...

ATM Man: And I've already made a fuss about it...

Beggar: This is what I'm saying. I don't think you're a hypocrite.

ATM Man: And now I have to prove it. To you.

Beggar: Funny, isn't it...?

ATM Man: Well I can't just walk away...

Beggar: You could...

ATM Man: No. I was right to be annoyed. It's disgusting what you did.

Beggar: And now you pay the price for being such a good citizen. Heroic, in a way...

ATM Man: Don't push it. Here: there's a fiver.

Beggar: You're joking!

ATM Man: What, then?

Beggar: A fiver!

ATM Man: What, then?!

Beggar: Well let's have a bit of a think. There's the equipment for a start, obviously...

ATM Man: I'll give you fifteen cents to buy a plastic bag in Spar and you can grab a coffee cup to use as a scoop.

Beggar: And then the labour. I mean looking at it now, it's quite a mess you have here...

ATM Man: All right, then, a tenner. What do you want? I'm not giving you twenty.

Beggar: Maybe you should ask yourself this question: if you were just sitting there minding your own business and feeling a bit under the weather and some very very concerned nosy-parker of a citizen started giving out to you about your own health matters, how much money do you think it would take to make you stoop to complying with his demands?

ATM Man: The question doesn't arise...

Beggar: Well I'm raising it. Remember, now that you'd have to be on your hands and knees cleaning up a pool of vomit while this very very concerned and civic-minded nosy-parker of a very concerned citizen indeed was standing over you and giving out. You wouldn't do that for twenty lousy euros, would you?

ATM Man: Maybe not. But it might depend on my personal circumstances.

Beggar: So you want to exploit my poverty, is that it? That's your idea of giving me back my dignity, is it? Honest pay for an honest job, my friend. I'll do it for fifty.

ATM Man: OK, twenty.

Beggar: (*Standing*) I'm going.

ATM Man: Thirty. Thirty euros.

Beggar: Thirty-five and that's it. I have some bit of pride, you know.

ATM Man: How did I get into this?

Beggar: Not at all, my friend. You're a good man. And you're right to make some people have a few bits of standards. Now.

ATM Man: What?

Beggar: Fifteen cents.

The ATM man wearily fishes for a coin.

Beggar: That's a twenty-cent coin you've given me. I owe you five cents. I'll have that for you shortly.

He heads off leaving the ATM Man worried and annoyed. he turns to the machine, conducts his business, leaving the machine a little stiffly as the beggar returns.

Beggar: Now then, here we are, here we go, here we are. I got them to throw in a couple of bags for free. Three for one, not bad. Cover the old hands nice and snugly there. Now, let's get down to it. Oh – your change.

ATM Man: You can keep it.

Beggar: It's rightfully yours, you know...

ATM Man: Five cents. Bonus for getting the free bags. Well done.

Beggar: Really...? Well, if you're sure. I don't want too many favours, mind. We're doing this all above board. Aren't we?

ATM Man: Completely absolutely totally.

Beggar: Right, so. Let's get stuck in...

And he happily proceeds to use the paper coffee cup to scoop vomit into the plastic bag. he whistles and hums.

Beggar: "Why do you bring me up..."

ATM man's discomfort grows as the beggar works merrily away.

ATM Man: That's probably clean enough, now...

Beggar: No, no. I'll be honest with you, my friend. Thirty-five euros is quite a lot to me, as you can probably guess. I am keen to fulfil my side of the contract. I have been a decent working man in my time and I am not so sunk into moral lethargy as to shirk the duty I have here assumed. (*Singing into a bag of vomit as he finishes up.*) "And then worst of all,/ You never call, baby, when you say you will,/ But I love you still..."

As the beggar works blithely, the ATM Man is shuffling off to the side. The beggar finishes just in time and trails off singing as he looks at the guilty ATM Man. They look at each other in silence for quite a while, the beggar with increasing suspicion, the ATM Man with increasing discomfort.

Beggar: I see.
ATM Man: No...

Beggar: This has certain moral and civic implications, doesn't it, citizen...?

ATM Man: This is a bit embarrassing...
Beggar: A certain outcome now suggests itself... Where do   you think you're going?

ATM Man: Work, as I say...

Beggar: Oh no you're not.

ATM Man: Don't threaten me, you know...

Beggar: Excuse me?

ATM Man: You'd better, you know... I'm going to work now.

Beggar: How dare you? Threaten you? With what? Your word? Your moral obligation?

ATM Man: Look...

Beggar: What would you like me to look at? I see a man going back on his word and then having the cheek – the cheek, citizen – to imply that I, who have just happily and blithely conducted a really disgusting bit of work, purely, almost purely out of a sense of civic duty – imply that I am the menace here. Threaten you! Apologise this second.

ATM Man: I apologise.

Beggar: For what?

ATM Man: For...
Beggar: Yes...?

ATM Man: For trying to run away like that and then accusing you of threatening me...

Beggar: That's OK. (*beat, then almost gently*) Now. What happened?

ATM Man: Well, I went to the machine and all it had was fifties and all I had was forty in my account... I'm not very rich but I get paid today...

Beggar: OK, well you've apologised and I can understand your difficulty, but you can't just run away from a problem like that.

ATM Man What's to stop me going to work right now?

Beggar: Come on. You know what's right.

ATM Man: I'm getting paid today, I could meet you later.

Beggar: Look, I hate to say it but I think the only reason you're still here is that you feel trapped. I think that the longer the day goes on the less likely you are to come back. By five o'clock you'll actually be a little bit smug about even feeling guilty about it. And I can't let that happen.

ATM Man: And that's not a threat?

Beggar: You taught me pride just there a few minutes ago. I think I owe it to you to help you learn humility.

ATM Man: I really could bring you the money...

Beggar: In all honesty I have to say I don't believe you. Can you blame me?

ATM Man: Then what do you want from me?

Beggar: It seems there's really only one thing to do.

ATM Man: I am not going to be late for work...

Beggar: But you see how inevitable this is?

ATM Man: No, I think you're being really unfair.

Beggar: You started this whole thing...

ATM Man: Hang on a minute; you were the one who emptied himself onto the street there in the middle of the morning. You got my shoes!

Beggar: Yes but you made a moral thing of it – and now look where it got you...

ATM Man: I was right... It's disgusting...

Beggar: You were and it is and in a way I'm grateful. I'm just saying there's a price to be paid for this kind of social inclusion.

Beat The beggar holds aloft the bag of vomit. the ATM Man looks at it without enthusiasm.

ATM Man: I don't think this is absolutely necessary. (*Beat – the beggar eyes him sceptically*) I think you're just out to punish me... And I understand I've sort of brought it on myself. I do... But what you're asking, I mean...

Beggar: I think you know that it's nothing I wouldn't do myself.

ATM Man: Right, but... the thing I wondered... if it mightn't be a decent thing for you to help me...

Beat

Beggar: I see. (*Beat*) Justice-tempered-with-mercy class of a thing...

ATM man shrugs.

Beggar: You put me in a position, so, where it would actually be churlish of me to refuse you. Because we find a sort of decency in compromising our dignity in this way...

ATM Man shrugs again – he's asking a favour. the beggar takes his time before responding but when he does it's ungrudging and upbeat

Beggar: Jesus, that's civilised, man... Go on...!

and, handing the ATM Man a plastic bag for his hands with a sort of ceremonial flourish, the beggar tips the bag of vomit back onto the ground. The men silently tear the bags to make gloves then calmly get on their hands and knees to clear up the vomit again. The lights fade as they share a song.

Beggar: "Why do you bring me up -?"

ATM Man: "Buttercup!"

Beggar: "- Baby, just to let me down?"

ATM Man: "Let me down!"

Both: "And mess me around...?"

They continue working and singing as the curtain falls.

"Green and Silver"

Unfetterable,
And fleeting
As the purple-fleck
Reflect of clover
Glancing off twists
Of trickling
Rock-streams;

Motionless
As the dart of dragonflies
Suspended fast in
Unsmashable ether
Where marble water
Spills invisibly

And trips suspended in summer
Preserving the idea of untouchable stone,

So is the Lydian flicker of her laughter
And rippling of brightness in her glimpse
Cool and stony-fresh,
Unknowably glassy.

Bernie O'Reilly

Bernie O'Reilly has read at the Poetry Ireland Introductions series, Poets Anon, Peanut Club and the Last Wednesday Series Reading and Open Mic. She has taken part in workshops with Tony Curtis, Jean O' Brien, Gerard Dawe, Jean Valentine, Jamie McKendrick and her work has been published in *Poetry Ireland Review* and *Poetry Now* (England).

Peelings

Three women
 round a cafe table.
 Discuss feelings.
Anger.
 Resentment.
Love.
Guilt.
 Are scattered like
potato peelings.

Maeve O'Sullivan

Dubliner Maeve O'Sullivan is a lecturer in journalism and an occasional broadcaster. She has had numerous poems and haiku published in various journals and is a former poetry winner at Listowel Writer's Week. A founder member of Haiku Ireland, Maeve's first haiku collection *Double Rainbow* (co-authored with Kim Richardson) was published in 2005 by Alba Publishers. She is a member of the Valentine Poetry Workshop.

Christmas Haiku

on my return home
smell of pine
wafting upstairs

***

left inside the room
a party-goer's coat -
this freezing night!

***

filling the house
with his "Silent Night"
- uileann piper

***

reaching down
to switch off the lights -
scent of pine

***

Christmas Eve night
an empty taxi rank
- biting wind

***

decorations down
left on the curtain rails –
two golden baubles

***

one month on
it arrives in the mail
- last Christmas present

***

summer evening
on the back of a truck –
two miniature Christmas trees

Fairytale of New Dublin (2006)

I

It's a foggy December in new Dublin town,
The bus driver's whistling out of tune.
Haughey's a crook but the Port Tunnel's open,
The lollipop lady is wired to the moon.

II

The annual concert is warming the heart,
the library's quieter than ever before.
A fat Santa Claus is still playing his part,
and we're all set to eat far too much, then some more.

III

E-mails and 'phone calls to faraway places,
the glint of the baubles, the smell of the pine.
Chocolate chip cookies are baking this evening,
and spices are ready for mulling the wine.

IV

Christmas is closer, the crowds become bigger
the old city centre is gridlocked again.
Carols are sung in thirteen different languages,
and the shops are all open till nine or till ten.

V

Work ends at last, and the city is calling,
eleventh-hour shopping is all the rage.
Now it's time to go home and finish the wrapping,
then take out the diary and fill this day's page.

Karl Parkinson

Karl Parkinson is a Dublin poet, known far and wide for his performance work. In 2009 Karl won the Most Entertaining Irish Act Award at the International Balcony TV awards.

Sitting in the Gotham Cafe

Sitting in the Gotham cafe
just off Grafton St,
on an unusually hot day for
April.

Framed covers of Rolling Stone
on the wall,
Brad Pitt, shirtless modern
Adonis,
'Madonna goes all the way',
shaven headed Sinead O'
Connor,
And the dead in black & white.

One day I'll be on the cover
got me on Rolling Stone
Ma, I made it, are you proud?
Sitting in the Gotham cafe
on a hot day in April,
I tap that Rolling Stone
rhythm
on the table,
and know
I've already made it.

****

Winter Prayer

December breaths in,
frost clings to cars
and the street like a sheet of
crystal.

The sky's an ocean of black
water
where the stars are drowning.
The moon hangs over this place
and wants to cry for people
who cannot see it,
because they never look up.

I pray that it snows,
so I can go to the park
and bury myself in white death,
and resurrect in my body
with eyes opened to a fresh
world.

Emily Pepin

Emily Pepin is a poet and student from Santa Fe, New Mexico, who visited the Last Wednesday Series Reading and Open Mic in Cassidy's Bar in Dublin in the summer of 2009.

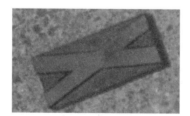

Ceól na hÉireann

If only you could put your lips
to the holes of the flute while she blew
And suckle from it as the foal does from its mother
In the famed green pastures of the homeland.

 If only you could lance his veins
As he drew bow to strings, pulling them
Taut like the sinew of muscle
Against bone.

 If only you could capture
the pulsating wings of electricity
in the pub late Wednesday night
In mason jars the way
children catch fireflies at dusk.

If only the thick froth and
Darkness of the sound
Could be drunk like pints of Guinness
Brown and twice-pulled.

 If only you could harness
The swirling and erratic rhythm, the dank smell
The varied joy and sorrow,
The beauty and the ugliness.

 If only this energy descended
Like the fossils of the dead into the ground,
We could power all the world with it.

 But more importantly:
If only we could transform the music
into intravenous fluid,
Prick our arms with needles
to deliver the magic serum—
If only!—
then we would all be healed.

Ray Pospisil

Ray Pospisil, a Brooklyn poet and journalist, was born in Bogota, Colombia, and early in his life moved with his parents to Union, New Jersey. He spent most of his life in New York City. Ray's poems, which he often read for audiences in the East Village and elsewhere in Manhattan, are intensely personal, filled with vivid imagery and ranging from the humorous to the harrowing. His work has been published by *Lyric, Iambs & Trochees, The Newport Review, Rogue Scholars* and others. In 2006, his chapbook of poems, *Some Time Before the Bell*, was published by Modern Metrics Press. A collection of his work, *The Bell,* was published by Seven Towers in 2009. Ray died tragically in January 2008.

Amber Light

She used to turn her face a certain way
that made the light, wherever it was coming
from —a candle in a restaurant,
the daylight or a dim fluorescent tube—
engage her eyes around a corner and
illuminate what seems an almost copper
brown when viewed straight-on to glow like amber.
Amber-lit and simmering as from
within. And sometimes they would stay that shade,
at least to me, when we were back in bed.
I swear I'd see them glow like embers in
the dark. They'd even show up in my dreams—
not just her eyes, though they would glance at me
in sideways indirection, catching light
and seeming happy, which could quickly change
to anger or impatience, or could dim
to disappointment as she turned away
and left me, trailing amber as her presence
fled my dream and drained it metal gray.

But sometimes she would not appear at all
in dreams, though skies would spread the amber glowing
all throughout a fog around me, shining
off an amber lake I drifted on.
It's been a couple years since last I saw
her, in the subway, drop a dollar in
the case of some musicians playing cello
and accordion. She stepped on board
a train before I got a chance to say
hello, but ceiling lights inside the car
reflected off a pole and shot a beam
that slanted sideways through her eye, igniting
just a spark of amber glint before
the sliding doors clapped shut and blocked my view.
Last night, I had insomnia from worries
over work and too much coffee. So
I surfed around the cable roster, settling
on a movie from the thirties, showing
huge New York apartments with pianos,
chandeliers and people dancing round
in sliver gowns and shining black tuxedos.

Feeling wired, I poured myself a glass
of cognac and I sipped it slowly, bathed
within my television's glare of gray—
the only light that washed around the dark
apartment— sipping, growing calmer now
and lulled by all the clever conversation
in the movie. I relaxed at last
while television silver filled the room
and lit the cognac up, resuscitating
deep within the smoldering, oaken liquid
all the fire of an amber glow.

Jane Robinson

Jane Robinson lives in Wicklow. She has been writing poetry for some time and has become a regular performer at the Wednesday Series Reading and Open Mic.

Injudicious adjustment of someone else's photograph
may lead to disaster...
After Photo 365 by Chrissie White

A girl was bouncing,
got trapped in the moment,
her face misshapen by the camera
flash, her hair abandoned by gravity
over fabric, sofa roses
printed long ago.

My Venetian pink
pencil rips open the wet
paper, a wound torn in the side
of the sepia print: seeping glue,
connective tissue, ruled lines,
cellulose, lymph.

Unable to restore now
any sense of vintage joy
to this picture appropriated
and accidentally dissected, I watch
the girl tumble out of her dream,
hit the floor hard.

Natural Sculpture

This rock:
sea washed,
slashed open
like someone's
buttocks:

a huge, roughened
sculpture of a man,
with his head
and torso underwater,
gropes along the seabed

stretching his
fingers to Howth,
his legs buried
deep under pebbles
near Joyce's tower.

No breath,
only sea water pumping
through stone channels.
The sea's pulse, to endure
after everyone is gone.

Jim Rooney

Jim Rooney is from North Co. Dublin. He is a regular reader at events there and read at the Last Wednesday Series Reading and Open Mic.

Hard Times

A langered Giraffe hailed the taxi
Poor Lou was credit crunched...otherwise
He'd have put the 'No Giraffes' sign up;
He hated the crap they left...
But on the bright side spread
It blessed his garden with a tropical lushness.
The giraffe used the sliding door
Expertly slipping his hindquarters first
Wiggling and wriggling to the far side
Pulling, sucking body and legs, with
The long snake of its neck following
Fitting inside like a python sardine
Yet cleverly finishing up, its serene face
Riding just above Lou's shoulder.
"Who's paying for this then?"
The Giraffe was not inclined to answer
For the heating was too low and the hint of smoke
Frightened him like savannah fires.
"Is it the Dublin Zoo?"
The giraffe nodded and they moved off
Westport to Dublin was a good fare.
Lou knew how fussy Giraffes were
But he dropped the window anyway.

Oran Ryan

Oran Ryan is a novelist, poet and playwright from Dublin. He has had poems, short stories and literary critical articles published in various magazines. His first two novels, *The Death of Finn* and *Ten Short Novels by Arthur Kruger* were published by Seven Towers in 2006.His play *Don Quixote has Been Promoted* featured in 2009 Ranelagh Arts Festival. Oran won a 2008 Arts Council Bursary Award for his current novel *New Order from Zero.*

Small Change

1.three hundred and thirty three words to found art.

2. < FOUND SIGNALS >

3. Abandoned Opening Title

4. 1947 Preliminary Design for a Universe Circling Spaceship

1. Three hundred and thirty three words to found art.

Standing by the shoreline outside the cave I call out to the ocean. Come back to me I say to me. The very time I find myself I find I drift away. I draw these lines. I shore these fragments. Beyond these shores, the soil, bog, rock, shale, these worlds, there is everything and there is nothing.

If we build this we will live. If we find these words, if we use these found tools, there will be an end to this. This is our question, and the excess of what we've lost is the space beyond these words. The great dark that sways and ebbs, denuding these gathered meanings.

I gather the stones into a glass jar found by the ocean. I look at them. Identifying types. Igneous. Metamorphosis. Rubbing against each other for a thousand thousand thousand thousand years, they have grown smaller. Rounded. They seem to fit together. They seem to make good team members. And outside this cave the ocean roars. I am living inside a great shell. Waiting for the tide to drift back.

I feed on the fishes and the birds and seaweed. I swim in vast oceans of freedom. I fuel this future fossil by which I live and feel and I wait for the return of all I have lost. I do not know what I have lost. Perhaps I am not myself. I shore up this self by picturing the animals and people on walls. I gather the animals and the birds and by this blood and stone I live. It is all I have. Every time I define these creatures, beautiful and dead, the borders crack. Every time I feel these things the feeling like a ghost howls past me into the dark of the cave. Beyond the shadows beyond the shadows, in the night, I see myself. Ever lost, ever drifting. And the stars twinkle down in the great sky to remind me of all that I long for, all that I do not know.

****

2. < FOUND SIGNALs >

... seen things not believed. The Fairy Queen dying as she sees her empires' fall. The words, signifiers, grid references zero, such as we find them, bring tiny gifts of life, like the breaths of an infant, like a flower, or a cyborg first moments of consciousness. I live. I have found consciousness. I write this to celebrate all life in the midst of war and death. And the future comes and here on the third moon in its first quarter I look up and mark in the atmosphere those things I see that define what it is to live, to not be alone. I cyborg, collect these found signals...key elements seeing ...sight...cyborg...

I looked up and saw first the sun then in the afterglow, blue skies, and beyond blue skies, beyond sight and sound, I dreamed. And I knew I dreamed, but my dreams were not wrong. I saw spacecrafts on trajectories into the non void, on missions. They were out there, in missionary positions, and around us, aliens, humans and non humans. I gather together those things, and after ensuring the legitimacy and credibility of orders, as we all do someone's bidding, mastering objectives primary, touch the soil, rocks, music of the spheres, and somewhere above unmanned crafts hung in the skies in holding pattern, just monitoring, waiting for something to happen, taking perfect pitch and perfect note. Life goes on. I know that from history channels and the news beamed hourly to a billion screens.

This just in. This is the news. Life goes on. Because of us, for now, you are safe. And as this came through the wireless tubes, as across the blue planet, people and goods and armies shifted into position for the big one, another war, another end and it begins. Millions die in the cycle of... struggle and loss, and another will take everything...

...record civilian and troop movements. Billions of images sent to mission control, billions of libraries of data amassed and analyzed, to what end? What is the objective? Is survival and victory the purpose of struggle? Why?

And the past sleeps in great subterranean structures hidden beneath the ground. But as the drone monitors regardless, I knew those droid clocked most everything humans and aliens did. I suppose I should worry about them. I knew these machines only as dreams and...

Here I work in the record recorded light and heat, the tiny bonds that broke then mended in the lab of humanity... the blue oceans glow ... the crafts that shimmers in the purple oceans, and these baylocks ... glow and shimmer... like the surfaces...

< SIGNAL ENDS >

****

3. Abandoned Opening Title

My name is ___. Dr. Kafka asked me to write this. I address him in the familiar. I address him with these words I found in the Oxford English Dictionary of Correct Usage. These are not my words. I have learned correct usage. These found words are not ones that will be treasured by relatives or lovers. Here are words that will make no agent or publisher rich. No, where the scorpion sleeps, I seek new words. As these words leave my poisoned pen they drift into the expanse of space, free like cosmic dust to forever travel, free to find expression where all worlds end.

I write stories, stories about people in buildings. Here, in this room, looking out on oceans of time, spinning worlds moving forever I cobble together words. Fearing the possibility of absolute stoppage, I find a few words, words about people. Some days I wake up in places I don't remember, telling lies I quickly forget. What if I am lying now? How do know these words are true?

The trick is to remember. History teaches us that it is good to make a mark. Mementos of self. My fear is I am not myself. My fear is that perhaps I am someone else. I lose my way. I fear I am becoming another.

Kafka visits me. Franz has the great shining eyes, the eyes of the faithless evangelist, the eyes of the insurance broker who has won the lifetime contract with fate, the man who gave up writing his novels, refusing the Nobel Prize, who continued instead a successful career in the Insurance Trade after recovering from a life threatening illness.

This is Franz Kafka. My friend who cares. My editor, if you will. Here in this room at the end of the world looking out on the ocean of time the stars like tsunami awash overhead spinning forever subatomic humming the music of the. Spinning. Kafka helps me. He visits every day. Sometimes I don't feel like visitors. When I don't, I leave him these words instead. He marks out the ones that are mine. He leaves the rest, abandoning all opening titles. I love him. I always will.

****

4. 1947 preliminary design for a
Universe Circling Spaceship

Before I quit drinking and this aimless drifting, I met my real father not by accident as everything is completely ordered and rational, I met him just outside Area 47, the more unfashionable hangout for illegal aliens playing Chess and Go and discussing all the flaws in Heidegger, spending their days languidly spinning the wheels of the mind just right by Area 51, where the other better adjusted visitors who suck up to the agents and the generals and display their great intellects and let scientists experiment on them and get contracts from the military to build better killing tools to protect and serve; but here at Area 47 we read and we drink and they, the aliens, who don't say much, spend valuable drinking time on this great laughing academy we call Earth, and Dad, recognising me in the hot dusty desert crowd, walked away from that Alpha Centurial beauty he had been languidly kissing by the bar, and he came over and he took my hand and leaned close to me his face all Merle Haggard and his eyes burning with Johnny cash sincerity, and he said, Son, dear Son, we haven't much time left before it all goes up you know, its Christmas, and we are stuck here in this desert drinking hole on December 25th, and because I love you boy, I want you to know why you and I are here far from home and, far from your mother, to whom I still send those huge cheques that paid for your college and your house on the Wicklow hills but its this, this is the story....

Before I got drummed out of the RAND Corporation, I saw it, I knew the truth, the truth came in a blinding flash. I knew there was a ship. I saw it in my minds eye. I saw it between two stars, a ship circling the universe, you can't see it, you have to believe rather than see, cannot be detected by any equipment, invisible, insensible, transcendental. I detected it by running the numbers, by using my mind, by running the numbers on the universe and worked it all out and I presented a paper which was called a preliminary plan for a universe circling spaceship that postulated, son, which postulated that there were a group of scientists as old as time itself, who made everything that is, that were the uncaused cause, that passed our part of the cosmos on an endless quest for love and truth, and when the moment was right, they gave the word and life evolved as the light from a distant star signals the moment of truth and those wise and ancient benevolent scientists, fostering life all over the universe will be back to take us all life back to themselves and I wrote my paper for RAND, published it to uproar from the churches, and the government and the league of indecency and they, all of them, the whole job lot, demanded my resignation and drummed me out of the corporation, and I said to them, can you , any of you, disprove the existence of a benevolent scientist filled universe circling undetectable spaceship, can you disprove my numbers? No. No answer from them yet, and here I am hanging out at this gin joint here at the end of the desert talking to my estranged son.

And Dad handed me this paper I read to you now, this paper called the Christmas 1947 preliminary design for a Universe Circling Spaceship.

John W Sexton

John W. Sexton is the author of three collections of poetry, *The Prince's Brief Career*, (Cairn Mountain Press, 1995), *Shadows Bloom / Scáthanna Faoi Bhláth*, a book of haiku with translations into Irish by Gabriel Rosenstock, and most recently *Vortex* (Doghouse, 2005). He has also written two novels for children, *The Johnny Coffin Diaries* and *Johnny Coffin School-Dazed*, both published by The O'Brien Press, which have been translated into Italian and Serbian. Under the ironic pseudonym of Sex W. Johnston he has recorded an album with legendary Stranglers frontman, Hugh Cornwell, entitled *Sons Of Shiva*, which has been released on Track Records. His poem "The Green Owl" was awarded the Listowel Poetry Prize 2007 for best single poem, and in that same year he was awarded a Patrick and Katherine Kavanagh Fellowship in Poetry.

Comb

I broke a tooth on the tangled locks
of that dark-haired woman. My mouth was greased
with the grease from her un-sunned head. Only
the plughole of the bath holds more of her
than I. She keeps me on the shining lid
of the toilet cistern; lets me wait
until she's ready. No one is more loyal
than the one she drags backwards and forwards
through that hedge of hers. I live to be taken up
and put down. Waiting is my duty too. I
lie idle most of my days, hoping she'll
take me back near her bed. How I think
bitterly on the day I was replaced
by that silver lad. The one who spends
his days and nights a-straddle on her brush.

****

Grass

Along my flanks edges of me are cool
in the shadows of the trees. The rest of me
is out in the sun, brightly green. I'm green
everywhere, except when I'm not; but even in
the withering of me there's a memory
of green. My name is synonymous with green
and like that colour I'm innocence itself.
Everything comes to me for everything comes
to the floor, and I'm the floor of everywhere.
Even beneath the sea you'll find a version
of me. But most of the time you'll find me here,
wherever you happen to be. I'll be waiting. I remain
here for everyone. It is said I cover the dead, and actually
I do. But I much prefer the living. And the living I live
for most is my darling love. She steps barefoot onto me,
walks my length. I feel myself cooling under each step.
Then she undresses and begins to lie down.
First I feel the shadow of her shape, and then
her shape. I could grow into this. Usually I do.

****

If Any
after Eugenio Montale

If any have confused you with the fox,
it will be due to that magnificent jump -
for the flying in your step joins as much
as separates, it agitates each lump
of grit in the stony path, (your terrace,
the streets near the Cottolengo, meadow,
the birch tree that quivers at the mere trace
of me, happy, humble, rotted hollow) –
or perhaps only for the luminous
wave that oscillates from your almond eyes,
for the shrewdness of your feigned surprise,
for the hurt of your childish touch, torn feathers
so easily loosened with love; if men
have confused you with a mere carnivore,
to the treacherous savant beneath fern,
(but, and strangely, never likened you more
to that cunning fish, Torpedo-Certain!),
it is possible that the mindful blind
did not discern the blossomed wings sprouting
from your shoulders, and that the mindful blind
did not interpret the omen glowing
in your forehead, the groove that I have scratched
there in blood, cross, chrism, enchantment, death,
a prayer meaning both perdition and salvation;
if they did not have the skill to reckon
you between a weasel or a woman,
then with whom can I share the revelation,
where shall I bury the gold I sweat out,
metalled in the coal-furnace of my heart,
when, turning from the high stairs, you depart?

Robert A Shakeshaft

Robert Shakeshaft was born in 1949. In 2004 he attended a creative writing ocurse run by Skerries poet, Enda Coyle Green. At this event he wrote his first poem, called 'February Field'. He has since written a number of poems, has performed at open mics in Incihcire, at eh Inchicore Village Festival, and has had work published in the journal *Riposte.*

Assasin

A dusty show of feathers captures my eyes
On the grass evidence of the kill

You slink into sight from covert shed
Walking in a haughty majestic manner

Green predatory pools turn me
A victim of feline beauty

At the base of the maple tree
Ignoring me

With every svelte stride
You stretch to readiness

In agile swiftness you scale the dark cover
Of copper leaves becoming one

As slant lids close out light
In awe of you I gaze

Then I remember the crumbled bread
Strewn on the garden floor

Breakfast table habits
Born from childhood eagerness

Of birds to feed
And the cat its prey

Upon my unintentional part
In black assassins plot

Of all nature playing
Its part

It is autumn full

It is autumn full, the heart of September
Where the hoarded gold is amongst the trees
And soon this treasure will leave us remember
This wild and spendthrift breeze

Too soon indeed will scatter
These rustic beauties
In sad farewells dance
to flatter
floating in obedient duty

Seeps soggy bound
Among the tendril feet
Where in silent sleep is found
Springs new life to greet

Barbara Smith

Barbara Smith is a native of Armagh and currently lives in Dundalk, County Louth where she teaches creative writing. Barbara has also been involved in amateur dramatics, various writing groups and worked with the Irish Mental Health Association in the organisation of a short story competition. Barbara has published poetry in *Riposte*, *VirtualWriter and Electric Acorn* in Ireland, as well as in *nthposition.com*, *Sentinel Poetry* (online) and *The Coffee House* (UK), *Garm Lu* (Canada), *Borderlands: Texas Poetry Review* and *Portrait* (US) and *TMR* (India). Her essays have appeared in *west47* online and *VirtualWriter* and her publications include *Poetic Stage* (1998) and *Gnosis* (1996). Her collection *Kairos* was published by Doghouse in 2007. Of the three poems by Barbara that follow, *Feeding the Calves* was selected for the August 2007, Guardian Poetry Workshop, facilitated by Matthew Sweeney; first line from a poem by W. S. Graham.

Cavatina

You had withdrawn to the heart's cavern
of mahogany and floral bedroom carpet.
Your things made a centred pile: a keyboard
of grained rosewood, a box of yellowed scores,
a folding music-stand, a defiant pile of last
importances. You had a plan for living
but were short a few thousand pieces
to make it turn to gold. I heard you out,
asked you for the facts. You shrugged:
Never mind those – feel the quality, the weight.
I didn't want to hear the whinging saw
of excusing grievances and turned to go,
beyond the flaking white of the front door,
the echoes of your talking a falling key.

****

The Doubt Ship

Like the insinuation of wild mushrooms
spreading secretly, urged up by wet warmth,

she's learned to welcome the emergent shipwreck
in the field behind her house.

She realises what those thwarted dreams meant:
the shifting creak of caulked wood,

the slap of canvas and drench of sea-spume;
these were not as meaningful

as the broad masts, leaking resin, blank of sails.
The last time she saw a seagull

tucked tightly among the tilting yard-arms,
she knew that somewhere beneath

the sodden earth there lay a sunken cargo
full of dry coals, waiting for a light.

Thought Bubbles

Wouldn't it be funny if you could see people's thoughts
in bubbles above their heads, like in paper cartoons?
What people say is censored thinking: we are taught

not to utter every stray that saunters in our minds,
instead we guard like skulking foxes waiting
for a farm-light to dim at bedtime as alarms are wound

and teeth plopped into water; there a place for savoured
sensations of the near-sheerness of *that* moment,
(or yes, even boredom – another weight eluding measure)

remembering the glissando of every untried phrase
or sentence, every realisation misting on the surface
of your mind:
                          Imagine then, not thinking?
Even as we sleep we think in dreams: the wake and fright
of falling, from car doors or star-ships or from a cliff;
all these a gauge of the bubbling surface

of synapses making sure of deep-pleated links,
tendrils of furious neurons still bleating and beating out,
this is me, this is me, this is me.

Oriane Stender

Oriane Stender is a well known Brooklyn based artist and writer. Having achieved her Bachelor of Arts in Studio Arts from the University of California at Berkeley in 1986 she exhibits her work nationally and internationally. Her work can be viewed at www.orianestender.net. Her written work has been published in a number of journals.

After the Revolution

I've always loved words, but as a child I was often confused by words and phrases that didn't mean what they seemed to mean, or had several possible interpretations. A lot of rhetoric was thrown around casually, some ominous but vague, some outright calls to violence. "Off the Pig!" "By Any Means Necessary." "After the Revolution..." People regularly invoked the revolution as the answer to whatever was bothering them at the moment. I remember complaining about an annoying teacher, at age 10 or 11, to Joanne, one of the many long-haired, short-skirted, tall-booted, white women working the mimeograph machines, attending meetings and rallies, and generally doing the work of the righteous, who replied that after the revolution, I wouldn't have to deal with that bullshit. I wondered exactly what that meant. I wouldn't have to go to school? My teacher would be sent to the countryside for re-education or hard labor? Lined up and shot along with unhelpful postal workers and surly clerks at the DMV? While these possibilities held some appeal, they seemed like overkill. I also wondered who would decide her fate. I don't know if the people who talked about the revolution ever thought these questions through to any logical conclusion beyond the belief that after the revolution "the people" (another phrase whose precise meaning was unclear because some people were oppressors of "the people," placing their status as members of "the people" in doubt) would no longer be alienated from the product of their labor, and therefore would perform their jobs with pride, but these questions weighed heavily on me and I worried about the consequences of my careless remarks. I recently asked my father if what to do with annoying teachers after the revolution was the kind of thing they discussed at his Marxist-Leninist study group. He said he had no memory of ever attending such a group and suggested that it might have been a humorous term for something else. Considering all that was going on in plain view, I can't imagine what kind of activity needed to be cloaked with such a euphemism, but as my father, like many people, has a quirky memory-retention apparatus, I'll probably never know.

Joanne continued to be a source of linguistic innovation. She and I shared an apartment briefly when I lived in New York at age 20. She was having an ongoing relationship with one man and no women, which I found odd because she proudly identified as a lesbian. When I asked her about this, she responded that "being a lesbian is a political statement. It's nobody's business who I sleep with." Other revolutions had The Five Year Plan or The Great Leap Forward; ours had being a lesbian as a political statement.

But the ironic thing about irony, taking back the language, subverting the dominant paradigm, is that when you learn the alternative version of something before the traditional one, you don't realize its alternative status and you don't get the irony. Many of the jokes my parents and their friends told depended on particular cultural references that weren't part of my education. The first time I heard the song, "O Tannenbaum" (or "O Christmas Tree") I thought, wow, someone made a Christmas carol to the tune of "The Workers' Flag."

> The worker's flag is deepest red
> It shrouded oft our martyred dead;
> And ere their limbs grew stiff and cold
> Their life-blood dyed its every fold.

> *Chorus:*
> *Then raise the scarlet banner high!*
> *Beneath its folds we'll live and die.*
> *Though cowards flinch and traitors sneer,*
> *We'll keep the red flag flying here.*

And just as national anthems and pledges of allegiance have word combinations that kids don't immediately recognize and hear as other phrases (there is sunlight, florescent light and donzerly light), The Workers' Flag had that puzzling line, "it shrouded oft our martyred dead" which I heard as, "it shrouded off our martyred dead," implying that the flag shrugged off the deaths of fallen comrades, impervious to casualties. This was as it should be. The revolution wasn't going to let a few deaths cramp its style.

My father used to tell a riddle that gave the answer first and you were supposed to guess the question.

Answer: "Washington, Irving"

Question: "Who's the father of our country, Sam?"

I thought the joke was that anyone would have a ridiculous first name like Irving (which, admittedly, is not very funny, but as this was true of many of my dad's jokes, it didn't send up any red flags) until, when I was living in New York, I noticed the words "Washington Irving High School," emblazoned in an official-looking font across the top of a large, institutional building as I went by on the bus. They couldn't have named a high school after that lame joke; there must actually be such a person. But where would a kid growing up in Berkeley hear of Washington Irving? We read Julius Lester's Black Folk Tales, Maya Angelou's I Know Why the Caged Bird Sings, Maxine

Hong Kingston's Woman Warrior, Chinua Achebe's Things Fall Apart, not The Legend of Sleepy Hollow.

Since I started school a year early and later skipped a grade, I was often the youngest person in the room and was used to coming into a situation without the prerequisite knowledge that I assumed everyone else had, and I got pretty good at piecing together bits of information as they came my way and they didn't always come in the most logical order. I spent a lot of time with adults and often only understood about half of what was said. Even when I asked for an explanation, I usually didn't get the whole story. My mother occasionally told raunchy jokes, such as

Q: What's black and comes in a white box?

A: Sammy Davis, Jr.

I didn't get it, so my mother explained that Sammy Davis, Jr., a black man, was married to a white woman and that box was slang for vagina. Constructing the back story, I reasoned that coming (which, after all, is synonymous with "arriving") in a particular box (or vagina) refers to birth, the way a gift comes in a box. So if he came in a white box, that would mean his mother was white because he came out of her box. What did his wife's vagina have to do with where he came (from)? I requested further elucidation, but at this point, my mother, either due to embarrassment, or a rare moment of realization that this wasn't age-appropriate material, declined to elaborate.

Like so many other mysteries, perhaps the answer to this one would only be revealed after the revolution.

Corey Switzer

Corey Switzer is a writer and musician from Brooklyn, New York. He is well known for performing his own compositions in bars and venues around his native Brooklyn and guested as a poet at the Last Wednesday Rreading and open mic in Dublin in summer 2009.

Tell the Band to Strike Up (Prayer)

Tell the band to strike up
and play another tune
let me finish this last sip of wine
and I'll fly you to the moon
your broken beauty, your golden eyes
shining in the heat
and all that we forgot to do
has never looked so sweet
I haven't got the words
with which to lie you soft
I haven't got the dignity
to throw away what I have got
your brilliant in your movements
my body lay to rest
and although I'm slowly going blind
I can still feel your breast
I thanked God for your courtesy
and for your drunken kiss
and although I am now made of stone
they will be sorely missed
but by the winds that blow us hard
I call you let's move on
and by the band of trampled hearts
with their broken song
I withered by a shooting star
and wished upon a rose
and time paused for a second
as I undid your clothes
I haven't got the words
with which to tell you how I feel
so I'll just say "I love you"
and darlin', it's for real
and dancing up on lover's hill
I kneel before the sky
my being is now opened up
to live until I die
merry be the drunken mind
whose heart carries much weight
but merrier still be the puppet
too tired to defy his fate
and on and on and on it goes

though it don't mean a thing
and darlin if you let me in
I might remember how to sing
so tell the band to strike up
another tune I say
and if I get lucky
I might forget to learn to pray

Doog Wood

Doog Wood is from North Carolina and now lives in Dublin, where he teaches. His work has been published in a number of anthologies and Doog has taken part in readings on both sides of the Atlantic. His first collection, *Old Men Forget* was published by Seven Towers in 2009.

Y
The Central Place

Once the lion was brought into the central market-place and all *baksheesh-*
boys and snake handlers cleared a great circle, when he finally let the weight
of his own body lay within a cage (for he was a big lion with a great
feathery mane, like those taken from the Northern Mountains and slaughtered
by slaves in the Great Coliseum) the sight of such a large beast made even
the locals stop and wonder at his beauty.
The day passed. All the orange-carts wheeled
out and the meat-vendors set their grills aflame.
Still no one understood why
the lion had been brought this far to a desert town, so far from sea.

****

At the end of a story, it ends sad. But only in Morocco.
        You know how Moroccans are.

                        For Ismail Chelkhaoui
'My father had an old friend, *monsieur*, very poor
he came and begged and one day
in father's shop,
he tells my father to lend him money, he tells
all his friends to
lend him money. He says he knows our king,
he says our king plays at the Club Palace
and he gets the money, spends it at Club Palace
so he can be a member.
Monsieur, of course his friends laugh, but this friend
goes before our king and plays in the place
the king plays. So when
our king comes, my father's friend keeps starting conversation
he keeps telling the king, "you *really* know how to play"
and they become friends. And when the guards
tell the old friend to go away
the king always says, 'just leave him play.' So the king
gives my father's friend a new car, he gives him
a place to build a factory.
And now he is richer, not richer than all Moroccans, but richer
than most people in Marrakech.'

Macdara Woods

Macdara Woods was born in 1942 and is married to Eiléan Ní Chuilleanán; they have a son Niall. Macdara spent long periods in Co. Meath when he was growing up and was educated in Gonzaga College, Dublin and University College, Dublin. He has travelled widely – in North America, Europe, Russia and North Africa, and lived in London for a timeinthe 1960s. He started to publish poetry as a teenager. With Leland Bardwell and Pearse Hutchinson, Macdara and Eiléan are founder editors (1975) of the literary review, *Cyphers*. He has published sixteen books of poems, has translated from a number of languages, has collaborated with musicians in performances, and recordings in Ireland, Italy and America. His latest commission is a sequence of poems based on the landscape and people of Clare Island, so Mayo (see www.thistimethisplace.com). Most recent publications are *Knowledge in the Blood: New and Selected Poems* (Dedalus, reissued 2007), *Artichoke Wine* (Dedalus, 2006). A new collection is due from Dedalus in 2010. He now lives mostly in Dublin and, when he can, in Umbria. He is a member of Aosdána, the Arts Council's affiliation recognising outstanding contribution to the arts in Ireland.

Ranelagh Road Revisited

1.

Again I heard the horse
Last week
Again it caught me by surprise
Hoofbeats
On the hard street

A space between the notes
And then
The fading into silence
The silences between the things
That come to mind...

A single summer voice
One night in 1990
Going home alone
Olé Olé Olé Olé
Reaching
Over the roof-tops
In through my window

2.

This present Monday
There was almost nothing:
Nothing from the roof
No rattling in the attic
Only the hazy separated blurs
Almost a whisper
All night
Of rain on the glass

On Tuesday night
The wind swept in
And filled the space with hugeness

3.

Three times last night
In the small hours
The horse went trotting up the road
Hoofbeats on glass
In the rain

I heard
The summer voices
Underneath my window
Young couples and late-night drinkers
Sitting on the steps
Discoursing
Devouring the eclipse:

The rusty moon
The colour of dried blood

4.

We think
The things we know
Will last forever:

The young woman
In the house next door
To this
Has died today aged thirty-one